Literacy in development: a series of training monographs

Literacy in development: a series of training monographs
Series editor: H.S. Bhola, Indiana University

Learning to read and reading to learn:

an approach to a system of literacy instruction

Sohan Singh

Hulton Educational Publications Ltd.,
in co-operation with the
International Institute for Adult Literacy Methods
Tehran   1976

Acknowledgements

The IIALM acknowledges its gratitude to the Series Editor, Prof. H. S. Bhola of Indiana University, and to the authors whose efforts he has enlisted. Appreciation is also expressed to the German Foundation for International Development and the German Adult Education Association for organizing a meeting of literacy specialists to review this and other monographs in the series. Special thanks are owed to Dr. Gerhard Fritz and Mrs. Brigitte Freyh, Directors General of the German Foundation for International Development, and to Dr. Josef Müller of the Foundation's Science and Education Branch.

The cover design for the series is by Mr. Fred Zimmer. Mr. David Kahler of the IIALM has served as project co-ordinator for the monograph series. Spanish editions of the monographs are being published by the Editorial Magisterio Español, S.A., for the Oficina de Educación Iberoamericana for whose co-operation thanks are expressed to the Secretary General of the OEI, H.E. Rodolfo Barón Castro. Arrangements for translations into other languages are under discussion.

The material appearing on pages 46, 48–51 and 103 is reprinted with the kind permission of the Bong Mining Company, Monrovia, Liberia and of the Lamco Joint Operating Venture, Monrovia, Liberia.

Lastly, and above all, gratitude is expressed to the Government of Iran for a special grant which has made the series possible. In particular, appreciation is due to H.E. Mr. Safi Asfia, Minister of State and Chairman of the IIALM's Governing Board; H.E. Dr. Abdol Hossein Sami'i, Minister of Science and Higher Education; and to Mr. Fereidoun Ardalan, Secretary General of the Iranian National Commission for Unesco.

The International Institute for Adult Literacy Methods was established in 1968 under an agreement between Unesco and the Government of Iran. Its functions are to provide documentation, research and training services on methods, media, materials and techniques of adult literacy. The IIALM operates a documentation service and publishes three journals: *Literacy Discussion* and *Literacy Work* appear quarterly; *Literacy Documentation* is published three times annually. A Governing Board composed of representatives of Unesco and the Governments of Iran and Pakistan oversees the programme of the Institute.

Published in 1976 by Hulton Educational Publications Ltd., Raans Road, Amersham, Bucks., England, in co-operation with the International Institute for Adult Literacy Methods, P.O. Box 1555, Tehran, Iran.

Printed in Great Britain by John Gardner (Printers) Ltd.

© I.I.A.L.M. 1977
ISBN 0 7175 0765 3

Invitation to the reader

Reading a book can be like conversing with a knowledgeable friend. However, even the most well-written book is a one-way conversation. The author speaks and the reader listens. Sometimes the author anticipates the reader's thoughts and questions. Otherwise, the questions remain unanswered.

The International Institute for Adult Literacy Methods (IIALM) wishes to assist the reader of this monograph (and other monographs in this series) to engage in genuine dialogue. We live today in a world where communications between most parts of the globe are reasonably fast, most often dependable and not too expensive. We suggest that the reader send his questions to the IIALM—general and specific—as well as his problems in working with these materials. The Institute would be glad to help or to put the reader in touch with someone who can.

The reader should let the Institute know if, in his judgment, this monograph has succeeded in doing what it started out to do: (a) to emphasize that functional literacy programmes must observe the logic of the language of literacy as well as relate to the socio-economic needs which possess the power to motivate learners; (b) to emphasize the need for functional literacy programmes to achieve multi-level integrations, between reading-writing and arithmetic, between the three Rs and the subject matter, between student materials and the teaching materials; and (c) to elaborate an approach to a system of literacy instruction that adequately accommodates both these emphases.

With the readers' help, IIALM can indeed become a significant institution, an international correspondence college of literacy. There is the need. The address to write to is:

Dr. John W. Ryan, Director,
International Institute for Adult Literacy Methods,
P.O. Box 1555,
Tehran, Iran.

The structural and the social in the teaching of literacy: by way of a preface

A literacy project, whether it is traditional, functional, work-oriented or experimental, must include the teaching of reading. Teaching reading requires practice materials which typically are presented in the form of a primer.

For a long time, teachers of reading, and literacy teachers of adults who followed them, used the traditional alphabetical method in writing their primers. They began with the alphabets of the language they had chosen to teach; and spent long and weary days in helping their learners to recognize those alphabets. From alphabets, the learner went on to syllables and then on to simple words. More difficult words, and longer and more complex sentences, were then introduced, until learners became independent readers.

Learning to recognize the alphabets of a language often took long periods of time and the task was always tedious. The joy of being able to read was postponed for weeks and months. In the meantime, motivations to learn to read and write were somewhat dampened. In the school setting, children could simply be asked to come to school every day and to stay in classes. Children in schools have always been a captive group. However, adults who came to literacy classes could not be ordered to stay and dutifully return to the literacy class on the following day. Learning the alphabet, and the long wait in learning to read, were boring to most adult learners. The matters became worse when even the words and sentences that were taught to adults in literacy classes were childish in content.

As early as the middle 1920s, reading researchers had come to an important realization that had significant consequences for the teaching of reading both to children and adults. The realization was this: we come into this world as infants who cannot even mumble and we grow up to be

7

young people who make the most competent use of our particular mother tongues. In this process of learning to speak a language, we never see alphabet charts. Some of us do not even know that languages are supposed to have alphabets or even words. Reading researchers surmised that we should perhaps 'learn to read' as we 'learn to speak'. That is, we should learn to read words and sentences and particularly those that have experiential meanings and offer built-in motivations to us as learners.

This break with the alphabetical tradition has led to a multiplicity of approaches to the teaching of literacy—word methods, sentence methods, paragraph methods and eclectic methods. This has happened in all languages of the family of man. Now, since literacy workers could choose their own words and sentences and build their own themes, they could make literacy socially or economically functional. They could make literacy humanistic and they could make it political. We did indeed come to have functional literacy methodologies, work-oriented literacy methodologies, humanist approaches and, finally, a pedagogy of the oppressed—a dialogic approach leading to literacy with self-awareness and conscientization, the development of political consciousness.

The field of literacy methodology has, like most other fields, produced its charlatans who dub every primer a new method, and every little departure from the typical classroom setting an eventful innovation. It has also produced its enthusiasts who have left to the motivation inherent in the socially significant theme, the linguistic burdens it cannot carry. Some of the enthusiasts have forgotten that, for spoken languages to be committed to writing, those languages had to be *structured*—into sentences, words, syllables and alphabets; that once a language became a written language, it acquired a logic and structure of its own which now must be taken into account in the teaching of reading in that language. That is, linguistic structures and the motivation in the socially significant theme must both be respected in developing literacy instruction. We must make use of both the structural and the social facts in learning to read.

Sohan Singh, in his monograph *Learning to read, and reading to learn: an approach to a system of literacy instruction,* suggests an approach to literacy teaching that strikes a happy balance between the need to structure and the need to motivate in the teaching of reading to adults. He goes further than merely proposing a method of literacy teaching; he proposes a comprehensive system of literacy instruction. The system seeks to accommodate the needs of adult learners on the one hand and, on the other, of literacy teachers, monitors, literacy supervisors, forum leaders and extension workers who undertake various teaching and extension tasks in a functional literacy project. Again, the author brings out the need to provide instructional materials, both for learners and teachers, dealing with reading, writing, numeracy, attitude change and economic skills.

The monograph in proposing a substantive methodological approach to literacy instruction also demonstrates how a particular methodological orientation was systematically operationalized into a system of instruction. In that sense, the monograph is not only a prescription but also a model for developing different situation-specific and language-specific prescriptions. The process implicit in the designing of a system of literacy instruction is a typical instructional development process. Sohan Singh suggests that we start with a delineation of programme objectives; that these objectives be defined into separate tasks that have to be performed for the realization of these objectives; that a suitable division of labour between students and teachers, between teachers and monitors and extension workers, must be developed; that materials for both learners and teachers must be written and tested; and that all this should be done using the best that is known in the area of reading research and the psychology and sociology of working with adults.

His substantive methodology for literacy instruction is highly articulated. First, he asserts that, while teaching literacy to adults, the whole programme and, therefore, the whole set of teaching materials must be built around a theme of interest to the adults. This theme may be economic, socio-cultural or even recreational. Second, he distinguishes between two stages of a literacy programme. The first stage, he calls, *Learning to read*. The second stage is called *Reading to learn*. In the first stage, the emphasis is clearly put on learning to read. While a concern with the theme is still strong and articulated, the emphasis is on mastering the linguistic code. The structure of language is given due regard without neglecting the motivation that comes from the use of socially significant themes. Some 150–200 words which, in all languages, seem to be used 80 per cent of the time in human speech, are sought to be made 'sight words'. Attention is also paid to arithmetic, but at a very preliminary level.

In the second stage, the emphasis shifts to reading to learn. That is, reading is now used to get information out of written materials, while the learner strengthens his reading skills at the same time. Here again, the materials which are read are developed around the theme of interest to the adult learner. Any concerns about the structural aspects of the language become unimportant. Indeed, the methodology of teaching reading is now rendered marginal. The teaching of writing gets more emphasis. Also, the teaching of arithmetic acquires sharpened focus. Numeracy in today's world is an essential part of literacy and must be handled with competence.

The two stages of *Learning to read* and *Reading to learn* are brought into an integral relationship through Sohan Singh's model of teaching spirals. In a first spiral the teacher-learner interactions are built around a theme with emphasis on learning to read. In a second spiral, the learner returns to the same theme but now he or she is reading to learn and in the process is becoming an independent reader.

The approach to literacy instruction presented in this monograph should not be seen as a new dogmatism, though we do hope that this approach will be influential among literacy workers. Sohan Singh brings to his task decades of commitment and work in literacy with different languages in different parts of the world. For fifteen years, during the period 1947–62, he was associated in leadership capacities with the Ministry of Education of the Government of India, directing programmes of literacy, adult education, development literature and public libraries. From the Ministry of Education he went to direct the Unesco-sponsored National Fundamental Education Centre in Delhi and, later, joined the University of Rajasthan to direct the first department of Adult Education in an Indian University. Sohan Singh's long career in literacy and non-formal education culminated in Unesco missions on the Experimental World Functional Literacy Programme in Liberia during 1969–70, and in Afghanistan during 1971–74. His ideas, therefore, are worth more than a passing attention. He is systematic, but he is not the traditional alphabet man. In today's world where loud commitments to radicalism and humanism are fashionable, Sohan Singh's quiet sense of the functional and human must not be seen as conservative. It must be emphasized that what Sohan Singh advocates is not merely his opinion but is based on reading research and tested experience in the area; and, where he states his opinion, he has such stalwarts as William S. Gray on his side. We do, therefore, hope that the monograph will be influential in the organization of literacy work all over the world. Those who would choose to organize their work differently, we hope, would be challenged to clarify their assumptions and illuminate those assumptions using research and tested experience. We hope also that the monograph will enable us to define a methodological innovation when we see one and to evaluate innovative thrusts that appear in this important area of literacy instruction. Teaching of reading is, after all, the heart of the matter.

This monograph has obvious linkages with other training monographs in the series, 'Literacy in development'. A model of instructional development for use in the design of a system of literacy instruction has been treated at much greater length in S. Thiagarajan's monograph on programmed instruction. Edgar Dale in dealing with the teaching of words and ideas to adults will cover some common ground. Problems of producing follow-up books for the new reading public and of evaluation of literacy projects are also being treated in separate monographs.

We invite readers to examine these and other titles in the present monograph series.

H.S. Bhola

Contents

CHAPTER ONE

A system of literacy instruction: introduction to the approach

There is a widespread feeling among the articulate people of the world that literacy, that is to say the ability to read and write and do elementary calculation, is important for today's citizens. The feeling is seeping down gradually into the inarticulate, and even illiterate, masses of people. There are many reasons why these aspirations do not get translated into real literacy programmes. Some of these reasons are political and institutional, and some relate to a genuine lack of resources of different kinds.

Even when the will to eradicate illiteracy exists, some important technical problems must be solved. A large number of teachers, monitors, and animators must be recruited and trained to carry out any large-scale programme of literacy teaching. But more importantly, suitable instructional materials must be produced for use by teachers, monitors and animators who have assembled to carry out the programme. As a rule, literacy projects are unable to attract highly qualified teachers and related literacy workers to work in the villages, in the campo or out in the bush. This fact puts even greater demands on instructional materials. Instructional materials must then be so designed that they can replace well-qualified staff. The need to prepare appropriate reading materials for use in literacy programmes thus acquires crucial significance.

A system of literacy instruction

This monograph presents a comprehensive system of literacy instruction. It includes the teaching of reading, writing and counting. The proposed system considers the needs of learners as well as of teachers. Consequently, it suggests ideas about the preparation of instructional materials to be used by learners, by teachers, and by teachers and learners together. The

15

monograph begins by providing a rationale for creating a system of instructional materials for literacy teaching and describes how the rationale can be translated into the total family of instructional materials which can be handled and assimilated by the audience for whom the materials have been developed. We do not offer a rigid system but suggest an approach that strikes a balance between the need for structure, on the one hand, and the need to build upon the motivations of adult learners, on the other.

What do we mean by a system of literacy instruction? A system of literacy instruction may be seen to have four characteristics. Instruction has *comprehensiveness* without irrelevance; elements are assembled in an *order;* there is an *integration* of different elements; and this integration lends *unity* to the whole structure. Let us take these four characteristics one by one and see how they influence the design of instructional materials.

Comprehensiveness
Comprehensiveness is a relative term. What is comprehensive at the level of one system may not be so at another. Even at the same level, comprehensiveness has different facets. We must look at each man or woman who comes for literacy training and ask again and again: 'What level of skill is needed by the learner to function in a particular system at a particular level?'

Let us take the case of a housewife in a developing society who comes to seek literacy. Her major interests may include care of children, providing food and clothing for her family, learning to manage the family budget, and cleanliness in the home and the environment. She may also be interested in family planning, family health and first aid. Within these fields she may be good at doing certain things but she may fall short in others. A comprehensive and relevant literacy programme for her must include instruction in all those areas where she is inadequate. At the end of her literacy course she should be able to read the literature that she may encounter in newspapers and magazines. Similarly, her writing and computational skills should be sufficient for her needs in such matters as shopping lists and money transactions.

The test of comprehensiveness of an instructional system is that after her literacy course the housewife should need no follow-up course for becoming functional in the community in which she lives. Needless to say, this characteristic of comprehensiveness of instructional material is not merely a matter of quick tabulation of skills that the instructional materials specialist thinks are needed by learners. It will require on the part of the materials specialist an intimate knowledge of the cultural, social, economic, political, psychological and linguistic characteristics of the group of people who will use these instructional materials. Without a knowledge of these characteristics the quality of instructional materials would be greatly impaired.

Order

The second characteristic of any system is a particular order in the arrangement of its elements. Taking the elements of a literacy programme —reading-writing, computation and subject matter—order means that there should be a gradation of steps reflected in the system of literacy instruction and in the instructional materials parallel with the developing abilities of learners. In reading-writing, the structure of the language of literacy instruction and the introduction of vocabulary provides a basis for this gradation. In computation, also, there are well-established gradations that are dictated by the logic of numbers and mathematical processes. In deciding the order of subject matter we may have the option to pick our starting point but, having done that, we have to utilize the well-known formulas for gradation—go from the known to the unknown, from the simple to the complex, from general rules to particular examples, or from particular examples to general rules.

Integration

The third characteristic of a system is integration: the coming together of separate and diverse elements or units into a harmonious whole. Integration means the joining of one element of a system with another and the coming together of different elements in the unity of a process. This coming together—i.e. integration—is easily achieved in the matter of reading and writing. It is more difficult to achieve integration between the elements of reading and writing, on the one hand, and computation on the other. Integration is most difficult to achieve between the elements comprising literacy (namely, reading, writing and computation) and the element of subject matter.

In Unesco's variety of work-oriented literacy this has been a burning question throughout the duration of the Experimental World Functional Literacy Programme. The difficulty in the integration of reading-writing, computation and subject matter arises because each of these three main aspects of functional literacy has its own logic and no two of these logics may coincide. Yet, if a literacy programme and its supporting instructional materials are to have their appeal to learners, they must be an integral whole and not a confused collection of separate parts. Integration must also be achieved in another aspect. Not only the elements of reading-writing, computation and subject matter should be integrated in instruction, but also different varieties of instructional materials must be integrated into a harmonious package of instructional aids.

Unity

It can be asserted that a literacy programme has its greatest impact on learners if it gives them the power they seek in the area of their concerns. These shared concerns of a group of learners should be organized into a theme which should provide unity to the system of literacy instruction and to the instructional materials. We can assimilate something only when it has meaning for us, and something has meaning for us when its unity shines through its diversity. A musical air stirs us because it is not just a jumble of sounds but a series of sounds formed into a unity. In the same way a unity of theme must run throughout the instructional materials supporting a literacy programme. And the unity of theme in instructional materials can only come through the unity of theme in their subject matter. This unity of theme may lie hidden under the surface in some parts of instructional materials, but it must be brought out explicitly time and time again.

The delineation of an approach

In the preceding sections, we have discussed the four general characteristics of a system of literacy instruction. We will now describe how to design such a system. Before doing that, however, let us examine briefly the term 'instruction'.

What is instruction? Instruction is a binary term which suggests a donor and a recipient. A flow of knowledge and skills from the donor to the recipient is implied. Whilst instruction does include this flow from the instructor to the instructee, the process of instruction would be failing if it did not result in the learner's development as an individual. When an adult seeks 'instruction' he does so in his own interest in order to seek greater power for control over his environment.

A farmer may be concerned about a disease on his crop. What he needs is the power to eradicate this menace to his crop. The task of the instructor is not only to regulate the flow of knowledge from himself to the learner about the plant disease but also to provoke new actions from the learner which can remove the affliction to his crop. In fact, the adult seeking instruction is already responding to the elements in the situation confronting him. What he now seeks is more power in his actions. The instructor assists the learner to acquire this power. The basic philosophy of our view of instruction requires the instructor to allow the adult learner the possibility of developing and making more efficient responses to the situation of his life and work. Further, it must be possible for the adult learner to practise the newly learnt responses in an interesting way and to become used to the evocation-response style of learning. That is, learning draws out responses from the learner; it brings forth new capacities.

In an approach to the design of a system of literacy instruction we see two stages in the process of an illiterate adult becoming an independent learner. These are: (a) learning to read; and (b) reading to learn. In the first stage, the main interest of the learner is 'learning to read'; in the second stage, his main interest is 'reading to learn'. These two stages are

FIGURE 1. *The two teaching spirals of 'learning to read' and 'reading to learn'*

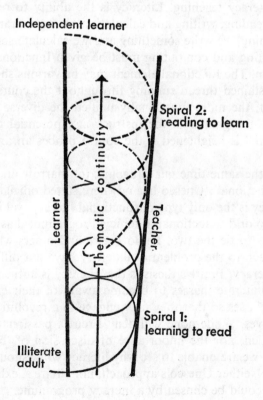

combined through two teaching spirals which are organized around a chosen subject matter theme. A graphic presentation of the system is given in Figure 1 and should be examined.

The journey from illiteracy to independent learning involves an interaction between the teacher and learner. The instructional process involves the transfer of knowledge and skills, and learner growth. There are two phases in the system: Spiral 1, learning to read; and Spiral 2, reading to learn. The spirals are organized around one subject-matter theme which provides the system with unity and continuity. The spirals overlap, the second spiral returning to the subject-matter concerns of the first spiral. We will have more to say about these questions and issues later.

Functional literacy

Questions about the unifying theme in a system of literacy instruction brings us to a discussion of functional literacy. All good literacy teaching is functional literacy teaching. Literacy is the ability to read, write and calculate. But reading, writing and calculation are not intransitive verbs— we read something, we write something and we calculate something. That is, reading, writing and computing must be given functions when taught in the classroom. The functional element may be various short themes, or it may be a sustained thread running throughout the course. Experience has shown that, the more functionally unified the diverse elements in a literacy course, the greater is the instructional potential of the course. And the potential is heightened if the course probes an area of concern to the learner.

We must at the same time guard against too narrow an interpretation of the term 'functional'. Unesco has nowhere stated officially that 'work-oriented' literacy is the only type of functional literacy, yet its very visible Experimental World Functional Literacy Programme has misled many literacy workers to tie the two. Paulo Freire and others who sympathize with his approach to the problem of illiteracy have put different kinds of demands on literacy. Freire's thesis is that literacy is authentic only when it enables the illiterate masses to become aware of their exploitation by the oppressor classes so that they may engage in a revolutionary struggle to free themselves. While none will deny Freire's passionate concern for the down-trodden, nor the importance of discussion of 'basic issues' in literacy classes, we are unable to see why literacy work should be confined to these issues. Neither Unesco's approach, nor Freire's, exhaust the types of themes that could be chosen by a literacy programme.

Before concluding this introductory chapter we would like to bring to the attention of the reader the variety of instructional materials that are available and could be used in literacy instruction.

All the communication devices, from the common to the sophisticated, could form the materials for literacy instruction. We may classify them as follows:

1. *Written matter:* (a) Printed, cyclostyled or reproduced in some other way. It may include charts, calendars, plans or diagrams of various types. (b) What the instructor may write on the blackboard.
2. *Spoken matter—Direct:* (a) What is spoken by the teacher. (b) A talk by or a conversation with a resource person.
   —*Reproduced:* (a) Radio broadcasts. (b) Tape recordings.
3. *Visual material—Two dimensional:* (a) Pictures, line drawings or photographs. (b) Diagrams, plans, charts. (c) Silent films, filmstrips.
   —*Three dimensional:* (a) Specimens of things actually used. (b) Models.
4. *Audio-visual material:* (a) TV programmes. (b) Video recordings. (c) Sound film-shows.
5. *Participative approaches:* (a) Demonstrations in classroom. (b) Field-trips and demonstrations *in situ.* (c) Drama and role playing.

Ideally, all the above types of materials can be pressed into the service of literacy programmes. But over-ambition is the sickness of professional educators. An instructional materials planner must think twice before bringing into the programme materials requiring sophisticated equipment and machinery. It must be remembered that large-scale literacy efforts are needed in developing countries and those very countries are too poor to provide for expensive teaching aids. Films—even filmstrips—radio sets and tape cassettes are often beyond their means. In some places even a blackboard comes as a piece of luck. The richer countries have often donated the equipment for some programmes. But, in the first place, the flow of sophisticated teaching aids is not assured at the time and place where teaching aids are needed, nor in the quantities in which they are needed. Secondly, even where available, such materials remain as decoration. As fringe materials they could be used, but then one must distinguish between fringe materials and instructional materials. Fringe materials are likely to be taken more as recreational than instructional, and may even be a waste of good time that could be otherwise utilized by literacy groups.

It is recommended, therefore, that an instructional materials planner should rely mainly on the following types of materials for organizing a literacy programme: (a) written material—printed or duplicated;

(b) materials which the instructor may write off hand, or as instructed to write in the teacher's guidebook; (c) spoken words, especially in group discussion settings which must always be given a prominent place in literacy classes; (d) pictures, diagrams, plans and charts that could be included with the written material which was produced separately; (e) specimens of things in actual use, if they can be assembled without too much bother; (f) demonstrations in the classroom, demonstrations *in situ* and fieldtrips; and (g) occasional dramatic elements, should the instructor have the capacity to utilize them. Implicit in these suggestions is an assumption: the teacher is not only able to use the materials effectively but also he himself has the power to wield this learning in the interest of his students. The assumption may not always be justified. We have seen that literacy is best acquired when it is combined with increasing efficiency in dealing with a field of concern to the learners. The instructor may, unfortunately, be deficient in either or both of these abilities—the ability to impart literacy and the ability to impart competency in the subject matter of the literacy programme. Instructional materials should be so designed that they make up for both these possible inadequacies.

Summary

In this chapter we have presented the four characteristics of a system of literacy instruction—comprehensiveness, order, integration, and unity. An approach to a system of literacy instruction consists of the two stages of (a) learning to read, and (b) reading to learn, integrated by two overlapping teaching-learning spirals built around a single content theme. The terms 'instruction' and 'functional literacy' were also defined.

CHAPTER TWO

Integration of subject matter and literacy

In Chapter I, we have pointed out the need for a subject-matter theme in a functional literacy programme. We also pointed out some problems of integration in the context of literacy instruction. We indicated that the three processes of reading, writing and computation—the three Rs—each with its own logic, needed to be integrated. The three Rs, together, needed to be integrated with the functional or subject-matter part of the total programme. (Subject matter would in turn include not only knowledge and information given in the classroom but also field work in agricultural settings, on-the-job training in industrial settings or other practical tasks appropriate to the functional theme.) Finally, the various instructional materials used in the programme needed to be integrated into a complete instructional package.

This chapter deals with the integration of literacy and the functional or subject-matter aspects of a literacy programme which, indeed, is the crux of the problem of integration. A lesson, as received by the adult, should be a composite whole. It should not only include reading and writing and discussion, but also illustrative materials such as diagrams, charts, etc. However, the concrete manner in which such materials can be integrated will depend on how the literacy and the subject-matter elements of the programme are developed. Therein lies a problem.

Before we set out to solve the problem as stated, we should be clear as to the kind of solution we are seeking. This solution is the discovery of a method of literacy instruction whereby the process of mastery over a subject matter—agriculture, craft or any other sphere of human concern—generates literacy. And the literacy thus generated is not merely a ponderous, atomistic 'decoding' of written or printed symbols, but constitutes an entry into the civilization of literacy. By saying this, it is not intended to soft-pedal the element of subject matter in a literacy programme. We have said that any authentic literacy programme must be functional, and a functional literacy programme which fails to teach the subject matter is false. But so, too, is a functional literacy programme false if it fails to introduce the adult learner to the civilization of literacy. As we shall see in the course of this monograph, it requires more than a set of instructional materials to achieve this binary relationship between the functional and the literacy elements.

Linear and spiral integrations

The linear method of integrating literacy and subject matter hands over the entire responsibility for planning the functional literacy course, and, hence, the related instructional materials development, to the subject-matter specialist. He proceeds from one part of the subject matter to another in a linear fashion and fits the requirements of literacy to the teaching of the subject matter. What does not fit, he simply chops off. The spiral method, on the other hand, regulates the doses of subject matter in step with the developing understandings of the adult learner and his literacy power, at the same time responding to the learner's work calendar. This may mean a return to a particular part of the subject matter more than once; but on each successive tackling of the subject, the adult learner brings to bear on it a greater power of literacy. This enables him to delve deeper into the subject matter itself. This method has been appropriately termed the spiral method.

We are dealing here with a dual problem—integration of literacy with the subject matter and integration of classwork with 'fieldwork'. In so far as the first part of the problem is concerned, writers like Paulo Freire[1], and C. Bonanni[2], insist that the subject matter is of greatest importance. This is to say, from the very beginning of literacy work, the gradation of literacy and computation is subordinated to the learning of the subject matter. In a unit of study of the subject matter, which may consist of one or more sessions, the adult learns some technical words so well that they become sight words for him. From these technical sight words the adult learner is taught to isolate the elements of the language used in the course. The learning of these elements then facilitates his learning to read and

[1] Freire, Paulo. *Pedagogy of the oppressed* (translated by Myra Ramos). Seabury Press, 1971. Also see Bugbee, John A., 'The Freire approach to literacy: review and reflections', *Literacy discussion* (Tehran) (Special issue, 'Functional literacy: one approach to social change', H.S. Bhola, editor), vol. IV, no. 4, December 1973.
[2] Bonanni, Camillo. *A literacy journey*. New Delhi, Indian Adult Education Association, 1973.

write the language. Similarly, from the very beginning the computational skills are also derived from the technical task before the learner.

There are two defects in this linear method. Firstly, learning a few technical words so that they become sight words does not produce reading ability. There are some common non-technical words, such as 'now', 'not', 'he', 'on', 'very', etc., which must be made sight words for making reading easy, meaningful and pleasant. Secondly, it is well-known in the psychology of reading that learning the elements of a language gives no assurance of learning to read it with comprehension, unless these elements are first met within words and those words themselves are set within a meaningful story. Further, unless about 150 to 200 words placed high on the frequency scale in a language (which would, of course, contain what I have called the common words) are made sight words, learning with comprehension would not result. Undertaking this task, which we assert is unavoidable if the adult learner has to acquire functional literacy, would undoubtedly mean rejection of the absolute importance of the technical substance of a functional literacy course. Similarly, computational language has its own logic which may not fit into the logic of the subject matter, unless the computational task is treated hastily. These lessons had, indeed, been learned from literacy work years before the drums of 'functional literacy' started beating. We can forget these lessons only at the peril of reducing literacy to a disjointed skeleton of itself.

Integration of classwork with fieldwork

The second part of the problem of integration of literacy and subject matter is this: apart from the integrated study of the two, is it necessary that both should be integrated with performance on the job or, broadening the concept of functional literacy, performance in real life? It is easy to see that those who give first priority to the technical aspect of the subject matter would say: yes. I believe that it will not take an educator too long to see the futility of any attempt to make two calendars coincide—the calendar dictated by the requirements of a man's job or the compulsions of real life, and the calendar of the pedagogy of literacy instruction. And yet, if we cannot bring our literacy to bear on our job, the functionality of literacy is seriously jeopardized. This problem of what I may call 'synchronization', of learning literacy at the same time as learning to do our work better, is without an answer in the linear method. It is soluble if we take recourse to the spiral method.

It is precisely in the vocational variety of functional literacy that the problem of synchronization, of translation to the field of what has been learnt in the classroom, presents itself in its most difficult form. An industrial worker's calendar or an agricultural calendar is seldom found to oblige the adult's work-oriented literacy class calendar. The agricultural calendar is the most difficult.

This came out in a very vivid form in the present writer's experience in Afghanistan. In the northern half of that country the land is snow-bound in winter and the farmer has no work to do. In the spring and the summer, he is so busy that it is too much to expect him to attend a literacy class regularly—should one be run for his benefit. In these circumstances, integration, in the sense of synchronization, of constant interplay between what is learnt in the class and what is practised in the field, was not feasible. The only practical course was to start the literacy course in winter and to include as much subject matter as the progressively developing literacy power of the adult would allow. This was the first spiral of the course.

Then in spring and summer, by which time the peasant members of a literacy group had acquired a modicum of literacy, the second spiral was mounted. In this spiral the peasants could come together briefly at crucial moments in their agricultural calendar to discuss, read and further discuss suitable written materials on the season's agricultural topic. Perhaps they could also receive reinforcement from visual and aural aids. They would then go back to their fields to perform the agricultural task with a heightened consciousness of its rationale and its technique and, therefore, with greater competence.

In the first spiral, the peasants were talking and learning of things which involved their occupational life, but the emphasis was on building up their literacy power, their reading-writing ability. In the second spiral the enhancement of their literacy power continued, but the occupational content was raised.

Similarly, in Liberia, where this writer prepared instructional materials for industrial workers, the first spiral dealt with general but basic concerns of the worker, such as industrial safety. This was done with an eye on teaching basic reading and writing skills. In the second spiral the worker learnt about the way to use different tools, and elementary skills in industrial or metallurgical operations. The improvement of the literacy power of the worker, of course, was not forgotten.

In order to integrate the spirals of literacy and subject matter, the subject-matter content and literacy content of a functional literacy course must be appropriately developed. We turn to the problems of developing the instructional content in the following chapters.

Summary

The various aspects of the problem of integration of literacy with subject matter in a functional literacy programme have been detailed. The linear approach to needed integration was shown to be inadequate. On the other hand, the spiral approach to integration of literacy and subject matter was demonstrated to be workable by the author's own experiences in the production of instructional materials in Afghanistan and Liberia.

CHAPTER THREE

Developing subject-matter content

We will now study some *general* ways in which instructional materials planners may develop the subject-matter aspect of literacy courses. The *detailed* development of literacy skills will be dealt with in a later chapter. This is so, not because we want in any way to soft-pedal the subject-matter aspect, but because, while the literacy aspect is a constant in all functional literacy programmes, the subject matter will vary from programme to programme. So that, in the very nature of a functional literacy programme, we can only deal with broad elements of the strategy in developing its subject matter.

The instructional materials writer is concerned with three elements in presenting the subject matter through his materials: (a) the dimensions of the subject matter to be included in the materials; (b) the exploration of the subject matter in such a way as to ensure that it serves to educate the adult learners; and (c) to write the subject matter into the materials so that it relates closely to everday life. We have already dealt with the aspect of comprehensiveness in an earlier chapter. In this chapter we will deal with the other elements.

Determining the content of the course

We will illustrate the process of determining the content of a literacy course by giving briefly the methodology adopted for the Farmers' Functional Literacy Programme in the Jaipur District of Rajasthan State in India. The development of the subject matter was undertaken under the guidance of Unesco's Camillo Bonanni during the 'exploratory phase' of the project, which may be stated succinctly as follows:
1. 'Identification through an opinion field-survey of the technical problems faced by the farmers, who are the future participants in the functional

literacy course . . .' was made first.[1] The *Teachers' guide,* produced under the same project says that this problem survey was conducted 'by a team consisting of a rural sociologist, an agricultural extensionist, a linguist and an adult educator. The information on the problems encountered by the farmers . . . was collected by interviewing, both individually and in groups, a sample of farmers [from the project area] and also by collecting information and opinions from district officials, such as the officers in charge of the national demonstrations, professors and lecturers in the Agricultural University, district officers in charge of education and agriculture, director and members of the staff of the Farmers' Training Centre, the B.D.Os, A.E.Os and V.L.Ws[2] of the concerned villages.' This team also collected 'Statistical data on farmers' population, together with information on their most relevant socio-economic characteristics. (Much of these data would be available in the Block office).'[3]

2. 'Confrontation of the farmers' perceptions of the problems with the diagnosis given by the agricultural and other specialists' was the next step.

3. 'Assessment of the real nature of the problem' thus emerged from (a) and (b) above.

4. 'Classification of problems by priority and selection of those among them which are *crucial* and *common* to the target group' followed.

5. 'Recognition of the linguistic patterns—philological, lexical, grammatical and syntactical—of the daily spoken language of the farmers, by analysing the texts of the group interviews, which have been recorded on tape during the opinion field-survey'[4] was the final step in this model of development of the subject matter.

The above description of the way an instructional materials writer—or his team of associates and investigators—should proceed to assemble the various aspects of the subject matter is, we believe, impeccable. Indeed the process of development of the subject matter should involve: (a) discovering the inlay of the subject matter in the individual and social consciousness of the group of adults to be covered in a programme; (b) investigation into the lives of the people, and recording, with their consent, samples of

[1] India. Directorate of Adult Education.*Preparation of problem-oriented learning materials—experimental project in Jaipur District* (1974). p.2.

[2] B.D.O.= Block Development Officer. A block, consisting of about 100 villages is the basic administrative unit of agricultural development in India; A.E.O.= Adult Education Officer; V.L.W. = Village Level Worker. A V.L.W. is in charge of agriculture development in ten villages in a block.

[3] *Preparation of problem-oriented learning materials,* op. cit., p.10.

[4] *Preparation of problem-oriented learning materials,* op. cit., p.2.

their conversations; (c) study and assimilation of documents and other materials related to people in that area and to their development problems available from official and non-official sources; (d) breakdown of the themes thus covered into topics and preparation of provisional instructional materials based on such breakdown; (e) testing of those materials with adult readers that represent those who would typically come to classes when they are opened; and (f) revision of materials on the basis of test results and other feedback. Of course, even this would not give us lasting instructional materials—for all times.

However, this comprehensive process may have to be reduced to suit the special circumstances of a literacy project. Such reduction may not always be done for reasons of limited personnel and finances in a project. At times it may be professionally unnecessary to go through all those steps. As an example, we may take the case of a Unesco project in farmers' work-oriented literacy, which was operating as a contributary to the agricultural project in Afghanistan sponsored by the Food and Agriculture Organization (FAO). Here the 'package of practices' to be 'sold' to farmers —the subject matter of concern to them—was already pre-determined by the FAO experts. The literacy team had to go by that. Again, some sort of literacy classes were already being held and there was an expectation from the literacy team that functional literacy work would start without much delay.

Under the circumstances, the reading materials specialist with the literacy team worked on the following plan: (a) existing studies bearing on the social terrain of the area in which literacy work was planned to be taken up were reviewed; (b) technical studies on the inputs needed to raise the quality and quantity of farm produce and the farmers' difficulties in mobilizing needed inputs were gone through; and (c) farmers were interviewed to find out what they knew and what they did not know about the processes that lead to improved farm produce. This, in Freire's terms, gave us an understanding of their 'real consciousness'.

These discussions were held with farmers individually and in groups and some were tape recorded. They also helped the reading materials specialist to come to know the farmers' linguistic style at first hand. The reading materials specialist then wrote out essays on various facets of the subject matter and had them approved by FAO specialists. Based on these, the instructional materials were written out and the main text was again reviewed by FAO experts.

Various types of tests and evaluation materials had been included in the instructional materials themselves. This provided opportunities to modify the materials as a result of experiences with the first batch of pre-planned classes. It was thus thought possible and, in the circumstances, advisable to dispense with the preliminary testing of the materials in a formal testing situation.

Including the subject matter in instructional materials

We will now consider the issue of including the subject matter in instructional materials so as to communicate the relevant information, attitudes and skills to participants in literacy courses. As mentioned earlier, we can deal with the problem only at a general level since the number of subjects which will determine the content of literacy courses can be as diverse as the interests of literacy groups. Within this limitation we will discuss three aspects of this particular problem: the *medium* or media of communication; the *form* of presentation; and the *order* in which the various elements of a subject matter are to be presented to the groups. The amount of subject matter to be conveyed to participants also has a relevance in this connection, but that has already been covered in the previous parts of this chapter.

Subject matter and media

In connection with the media of communication, we have to bear in mind the twin principles of the unity of communication and the success in modifying the behaviour of the participants.

In the first place, we should remember that all forms of language—speaking, reading, writing—are a unitary coding/decoding process and all forms of language must be drawn upon to mingle harmoniously in a unit lesson. Discussion provides an excellent setting for doing that. I am only voicing the general opinion of adult educators when I assert that a lesson in a literacy class must invariably start with a discussion. Discussion is a useful way of crossing over from the known to the unknown, both in subject matter and literacy. Also, being biologically closer to emotions, discussion is ahead of reading and writing in its productiveness. Finally, it can serve to fill the gaps in the subject matter which cannot be filled by reading and writing at the beginning of literacy classes.

Of course, the subject-matter proficiency of the typical instructors in literacy classes requires that proper instructions for the conduct of discussion around a particular lesson will have to be included in a manual for instructors. Other media will have to be used to carry the burden of communication. The reading part of a lesson will be taken care of in the text and the participants' workbook, while the writing part will be divided between the workbook and class exercises. Instructions should also be included in the instructors' guide for the teaching of writing.

An important variant of the reading and writing elements of language in some functional literacy classes is the reading and drawing of charts and diagrams. For example, an agricultural calendar for a crop is an important type of chart in farmers' classes. Also, diagrams can best illustrate sowing or fertilizing processes in agriculture, or making measurements in carpentry or metal-working classes. Hence, when we speak of reading and writing as media of communication for subject matter, these two aspects of language must be understood to include various types of charts and diagrams suitable for conveying the subject matter.

At the other end of the line of communication media are demonstrations involving specimens, tools, and methods and dramatics or role playing. These have the greatest potential in terms of behavioural changes. Role playing is often an excellent way of changing attitudes. Unfortunately, for most literacy classes, there is an unbridgeable gulf between literacy administration and the subject-matter administration which renders the use of demonstrations much more difficult than they should be. Insofar as role playing is concerned, specific instructions would also need to be given in the instructors' manual.

There are, of course, other audio-visual media that a literacy worker could use. Of these, illustrations in the literacy text are the most important way of reinforcing the text, of reinforcing and supplementing the discussion. Some would propose inclusion of illustrations in the text for their own aesthetic effect and for breaking the monotony of the text. Posters are good for starting discussions, but as learning aids they may not be as good as illustrations and charts. Another aid that could be harnessed for subject-matter delivery is a radio broadcast. However, an effective integration of literacy and subject matter on the radio still awaits to be done.

Forms of presenting subject matter
Various options are open to an instructional materials writer in regard to including the subject matter in texts for the participants. He could choose different styles—narrative, dialogue, self-learning materials, to name the most important. Self-learning materials in the form of programmed instruction, the use of which is feasible in literacy classes only

in its software form, seem conceptually attractive, but they are not always a success with the participants. Perhaps, psychologically, the materials are alien to their idea of education. In the beginning, the use of pro-grammed materials is awkward for them but, in cases where this initial problem is overcome, they are more likely to land directly on the answer through self-learning materials than to reach the answer via their own previous effort to tackle the problem.

Moving to the choice between the dialogue and the narrative, the dialogue has been found to achieve greater success with beginners in literacy. In the first place, dialogue materials can contain questions asked in a natural way and the question-answer form constitutes a good learning device. Second, in the dialogue words and phrases can be repeated without making the repetition boring. Such repetition, as we will see later, is an essential element in literacy materials for beginners. Third, the dialogue lends itself more easily than the narrative form to emphasizing the information to be communicated. Fourth, this form has the flavour of a personal touch and creates an emotional background more favourable for learning. And the personal touch can be enlivened by the introduction of humour and dramatic elements for which the dialogue offers more opportunities than any other form.

Insofar as the narrative form is concerned, we would like to mention one promising variation of it: to list the topics (which should not be too many), to deal with them in alphabetical order and, thus, make a simply written, mini-compendium of the subject matter for beginners. This form is, naturally, unsuitable for subjects like agricultural crops, where nature itself has established an order through a timetable. Nor would it be a suitable form during, what we have called, the first spiral of a literacy course, because of the constraints of sight vocabulary and lack of skills in the use of a dictionary. But I believe that, in a second-spiral class of workers using tools like hammers, files, etc., such a mini-compendium could be a very useful form of instructional material. For one thing, such lists need not be gone through from cover to cover, but topics of interest to workers at a particular time could be picked up and gone through.

Problems of sequencing

We will now deal with the principles governing the sequencing of subject-matter elements in a literacy course. Sequencing of literacy elements will be dealt with later. We may at the outset remind the reader of the distinc-tion we have made earlier between the first and the second spirals of functional literacy materials. The first spiral is aimed at imparting to the participants recognition of the more frequent words and word families and the fundamental computational skills, but without in any way departing from the principle of its co-equality with the subject matter. The second spiral is aimed at a freer treatment of subject matter, while maintaining the thrust for a greater mastery of reading, writing and computation. Within these parameters we will mention five principles of sequencing.

The first principle is that of interest or concern for the subject matter for the participants. For example, in the case of industrial workers in Liberia, this writer noticed that safety in the use of tools and machines was of vital concern to them and, hence, it formed the subject matter of the first spiral, whereas the proper way of using different tools was dealt with in the second spiral. Similarly, in classes for farmers in a multi-crop region, the most popular crop may be dealt with in the first spiral, while other crops may be treated in the second spiral.

The second principle is that of complexity of subject matter in itself, as well as its demand on reading vocabulary. To take, again, an example from farmers' classes, while the way of using chemicals against pests and diseases could be a subject matter in the first spiral, their preparation can very well be left to the second spiral. In general, there would be more detail, more scientific, social and practical content in the second spiral. For example, in a class for grape growers in Afghanistan, while the principal processes of raising vines were treated in the first spiral, topics such as the making of raisins and marketing them were included in the second spiral.

The third principle is that of chronology. In subjects such as raising of crops, where the timetable is laid down by nature, this principle is of particular importance.

Fourth, there is the principle of logical order. This order may be linear or collateral. For example, in classes for industrial workers, it may be necessary to explain the structure of a tool before explaining its proper use, for the simple reason that the proper use itself would depend on its structure. Taking an example from agriculture, it would be better to explain the nutritional needs of a plant before telling what particular fertilizers should be used to increase the yield of a crop. But, fertilizers such as urea require immediate follow up irrigation, which would suggest a collateral logical sequence.

Finally, as we have already mentioned, in some subjects the alphabetical sequence of topics could be employed with advantage in second-spiral materials.

Summary

This chapter has discussed how the instructional materials planner and writer can develop the technical or subject-matter aspects of the course with regard to: (a) identifying the various elements of the content of the course; and (b) the actual embodiment of the subject matter in the instructional materials. The technical content of the subject matter has to be developed through a process involving talking with potential learners, specialists, administrators, listening to conversations, discussing, reading documents and research materials. The process of creation has three aspects: choice of media of communication, forms of presentation, and order of presentation. Media used in a literacy programme to present subject matter may include group discussions, reading texts, workbooks for learners, instructors' guides, flashcards, live demonstrations and role playing. Forms for presentation may be the narrative, the dialogue and self-instruction. The special advantages of the dialogue in the first spiral was pointed out. Five useful principles for sequencing subject matter were learners' interest, simple to complex movement, chronology, logical order, and, in some cases, alphabetical order.

CHAPTER FOUR

Developing literacy content: teaching reading in the first spiral

By way of providing a perspective to the discussion of developing literacy content in the first spiral, some introductory remarks are in order on the content of the present chapter and on the content of the three following chapters dealing with: (a) the teaching of writing; (b) the workbook and the instructors' guide; and (c) the teaching of arithmetic.

The present chapter and the next three that follow deal with the teaching of literacy content during the first spiral. Since the processes of reading, writing and computing will be followed and indeed strengthened in the second spiral, some of the remarks in these four chapters will anticipate the problems and issues of teaching of literacy in the second spiral, to be dealt with later. Since the two spirals are supposed to be integrated, this should be understandable.

The whole rationale for developing instructional content (subject-matter content and literacy content) in a functional literacy programme as presented here is to achieve integration of the subject matter and literacy content. Therefore, again and understandably, some subject-matter concerns will reappear in our discussion of the development of literacy content in the first spiral that is the concern of these four chapters.

Finally, the integration of teaching reading, writing and arithmetic, as well as of the subject-matter content, must be embodied within some instructional materials. Therefore, a discussion of the processes of including content into materials often becomes a discussion of instructional materials themselves. This should explain why a whole chapter in this part of the monograph deals with the workbook and the instructors' guide.

We will now deal with instructional materials for the development of the element of literacy in a literacy course—not forgetting, meanwhile, that the literacy element proper cannot be disentangled from the subject-matter element. The literacy element, in turn, comprises reading, writing

36

and computation. Reading and writing are, in concept and materials, bound together more closely with one another than they are with computation. So that, for what we have called the first spiral, one set of instructional materials will be needed for the teaching of reading and writing, and a second set of materials will be needed for teaching computation. Though instructional materials for reading and writing will comprise one set in the beginning, we will, nevertheless, treat the procedures and materials for imparting reading skills and the procedures and materials for imparting writing skills separately for reasons of logical convenience.

In the following, we deal with the teaching of reading in the first spiral and the related problems of developing content. In the first spiral, the objective of which is to impart essential reading skills to pass from learning to read to reading to learn, the instructional reading materials will be of four types:

1. A well-constructed text which arouses and satisfies a real concern of the readers.
2. What the instructor himself writes for the learners, mostly on the blackboard, for the learners to read.
3. Letter, word and phrase flashcards to which the learners may be exposed by the instructor, to quicken their recognition of words and phrases.
4. A workbook which is primarily meant for writing answers to questions, but which also serves indirectly as a form of reading material. A workbook becomes reading material in the sense that, if not in the very beginning, at least eventually, the learners must be able to read the questions in order to answer them.

Before we go on to give a detailed view of the above four types of materials, it will be useful to state some theoretical principles which will help us towards a better understanding of the process of mastering reading and writing skills. For the time being we will mention five principles: (a) the principle of relation between speech and literacy; (b) the principle of establishing reading-writing responses; (c) the principle of maximizing the absorption of stimuli—that is written or printed matter—in one moment of attention; (d) the principle of alternation of exercise or concentration on work with rest and relaxation; and (e) the principle of rhythm.

The relation between speech and literacy
It is now clear that, insofar at least as literacy teaching is concerned, we should take reading-writing as a translation of speech—the translation of

one modality of sense data to different modalities of the same meaningful fact. Both speaking-listening and reading-writing are symbolic processes. They involve representation of facts by their cues, cues which point to the same facts for a particular social group and, hence, lead to a sharing of minds. In adult literacy classes, adults come with a fair degree of mastery over speech and we need not go into the process of learning a language. However, it is significant that in the new methods of teaching a foreign language to adults, learning to speak that language takes precedence over learning to read and write it.

Speech is a matter of the sense modality of kinaesthetics of the mouth region (lips, tongue, larynx), and listening is a matter of the modality of hearing. To the listener it is a cadence of sounds, distinctive for each language, in which certain types of meaningful patterns can be distinguished. Two of these patterns are important—the larger patterns of syntax and the smaller patterns of words, as stems or as paradigms. Of these, the word patterns are of translational equivalence of speech. The basic units of literacy are words, and the recognition of words—both in their stem forms and in their various inflectional forms—must be learnt to become literate. But, again, as words seldom appear in speech in isolated forms, but are invariably embedded in sentences within a meaningful matrix, so even the first words in a literacy course must occur in sentences in a meaningful matrix. A meaningful context may be technically called a story. So, we can say that all the words to be learnt in a literacy course should be set in stories.

If we liken words to recognizable parts in a melody, let us say the measures in it, then the musical notes in a measure correspond to the letters of which a word is composed. Now, it is not necessary to single out the notes in a measure to recognize it; the measures are recognizable as individual wholes. Similarly in reading, the words are not broken up into their constituent letters and then put together to read them; they are recognized as wholes. So also, in the teaching of literacy, at least the basic words in a language are taught as wholes.

Now let us take the same analogy from the other end. When we start to reconstruct a measure or a melody, we should know the notes and their sequence. The reconstruction of a melody is a form of higher consciousness of it, because it gives us a power over the melody, a power to reproduce it. Similarly, in writing, we reconstruct a word and for that we learn the parts of what we knew first as a whole. Writing then represents a higher literacy power, since it gives us the power to reproduce a word. The best quality of literacy is, therefore, produced when reading and writing are taught together from the very beginning. This means that, after words are recognized as individual wholes, they should be analysed into their component letters. The manipulation of letters to produce new words will give the literacy learner an even higher literacy power, the power to reconstruct new words.

We said above that speech has a cadence, a patter of flow and intonation. Sometimes the meaning of a sentence, or even a word, may be changed by a change of pitch or intonation. Try to see this by speaking to a person the word 'you' in a soft pitch and then in a loud and harsh pitch and see the effects for yourself. The second device of teaching literacy that follows from the translational equivalence of speech and literacy is to teach reading with the cadence and intonation of natural speech.

Another form of higher power of language is what we may call silent speech, the companion of the process of human thought. Corresponding to silent speech is silent reading which adds thinking to reading, that is to say, which leads to greater comprehension in reading. The third device of literacy, which follows from the translational equivalence of speech and literacy, is that the literacy learner must be taught to engage in silent reading, if not simultaneously with the start of learning to read, at least as soon as possible.

Establishing the reading response

We now come to the second principle, that of establishing the learning of reading and writing. If we take speech as the primary language function, then reading is a conditioned response to speech, in the sense in which a dog may be conditioned to salivate at the sound of a buzzer instead of at the sight of food. As we know, this conditioning is determined by the laws of frequency, contiguity and positive emotion.

Applying this psychological knowledge to learning to read: (a) the written/printed word, the recognition and comprehension of the meaning of which is desired, should be accompanied or immediately followed by the spoken word, the meaning of which in the existing context is known to the learner; (b) this process must be repeated at intervals, frequently in the beginning and gradually lengthening out; and (c) all this must be accompanied by a positive emotion in the reader. Positive emotion in the learner can be assured by providing him with the knowledge of results of his efforts. This may be done explicitly or implicitly—explicitly if the reader is told that the word has been read correctly; implicitly if the reader's guide does not interrupt him to correct his reading of the word. Reading responses are further strengthened if learning takes place in a satisfying context and environment, that is to say, if the matter being read by him arouses his interest and he is situated comfortably in relation to his guide and his co-readers.

Maximizing reading comprehension

Maximizing the comprehension of written/printed matter in a single moment of attention is another principle for teaching reading. It is well-known that, in the act of reading, the movement of the eye proceeds in a line in jumps and pauses. The jumps or leaps in the eye movements represents the amount of reading matter covered in one span of attention. The pauses represent the inner process of understanding, or comprehending the material covered in the preceding leap. If there is a failure in comprehension, the eye makes a reverse movement to go back to the material covered in the leap and makes shorter jumps and longer pauses. These reverse movements are called regressions. Thus, if the material is easily comprehensible to a reader, the jumps of his eye movements will be longer and fixations of shorter duration, and regressions very much reduced. On the other hand, there will be shorter jumps, longer fixations and very many regressions when the material being read is difficult or the reader is a beginner in literacy.

The length of the jump in the movement of the eye and the reduction in the duration of fixation is only possible if words can be recognized by a reader in the shortest possible time, when the reader is familiar with the subject so that key words can be identified by simple cues, and when the reader becomes familiar with the structural rhythm of the written/printed language.

When words are recognized immediately as a whole, they are called 'sight words'. Similarly, when short phrases are recognized immediately, they are called 'sight phrases'. When words and phrases become sight words and sight phrases, the eye movements become longer than when they are not and pause time is reduced.

In almost every language there about 100 to 150 words, which occur about 80 per cent of the time in ordinarily spoken language. Then, in every subject there are a few words and phrases which occur quite frequently. For example, if you are discussing about fertilizers for a wheat crop, the words nitrogen, phosphorus (or phosphates) and potassium (or potash) will occur quite frequently. Now, if these common words and key words in a subject are made into sight words, the process of reading becomes quicker. This is usually effected in literacy classes by the use of flashcards for words and phrases.

Again, when a person is reading a familiar subject some words can be comprehended by minimal cues. For example, when you are reading on what to eat, words like leafy vegetables, proteins, calories, etc., require minimal cues to recognize them.

The familiarity with the subject, the proper setting for orientating the reader to a subject, and the sensitivity to key words and phrases—which means comprehending them from cues to the general shape and length—are brought about by an oral discussion of a subject preceding the reading of it. When a person becomes familiar with the structure and rhythm of a written language, he can guess places where the key words in a piece of writing can be expected to occur, so that his eyes can even omit some matter—they can skip it, as they say—and yet read with comprehension.

Alternation of work and rest

The principle is well known in psychology that learning becomes quicker and more stable when periods of learning words are separated by gaps of rest from the learning task. The rest period, of course, must not be too long. Of course, in the very nature of literacy work for adults we cannot use too rigid and even experimentally ascertained optimals of rest and work. But, I think this much can be said that, for beginners in literacy, daily sessions, except for unavoidable holidays and days of rest, and sessions of, say, an hour and a half to two hours would meet the requirements of this principle.

Imposing a rhythm on learning tasks

Rhythm is one of the basic facts of nature, not excluding human nature. A rhythm can be imposed on learning tasks in literacy work with good results. The principle of alternation of literacy work with periods of rest is a type of rhythm in the task of learning literacy. But specifically, what we mean here is that in one learning session in a literacy group—which we said may last for one and a half to two hours a day—it is most important to maintain a rhythm between various types of literacy work, such as reading-writing and computation, and even within any of the two types. For example, within the task of learning to read, there may be a rhythm in revision of previous lesson, discussion on the day's work, reading the new lesson and practice in learning of writing in connection with the new lesson.

Reading text for the first spiral

We will now describe the type of materials necessary to learn reading. We will begin with the professionally built text for the first spiral of literacy work. As we mentioned earlier, the objective of the first spiral is, firstly, to establish basic reading skills; and, secondly, to cross over from learning to read to reading to learn.

Before we give the main principles of constructing a basic reading text for a literacy class, we would like to emphasize that, in writing the text, the co-operation of a linguistic expert must be sought. Even where the reading materials writer is familiar with the language, it is better to enlist the co-operation of a person who knows intimately the linguistic characteristics of the region from which the participants in the literacy group(s) will come. There are special words and distinctive nuances of words, which differ from one region to another for the same language spoken over a wide area. For example, in India, although Hindi is spoken over a large area, the Hindi of one region differs from its neighbouring regions. As the language used in the instructional materials for the first spiral should be as close as possible to the regional language, it is necessary that a person—usually a linguist with an intimate knowledge of the regional language—should be closely associated with the reading materials writer.

Building reading materials for the first spiral

The guiding principle in building up the first spiral reading text is to introduce a small dose of new words in each lesson. The first lesson, of course, will contain only the new words. But subsequent lessons would consist of a small number of new words and words already introduced in the previous lessons. All the words in a lesson, even the first lesson, should appear only in meaningful sentences in the context of a story. It would serve to heighten the visibility of the new words to the reader, and even the instructor, if these words (and perhaps also the new letters appearing in the lesson) are repeated prominently at the end of each lesson.

It is not possible to lay down any rigid rules with regard to the number of new words that should be introduced in a lesson, but it is the writer's opinion that on the average about five new words can be introduced in a lesson—less at the beginning and more in the later lessons. The earlier lessons may have two to three new words, while the last few lessons could even go up to ten new words. If a new word has an affinity to a word already introduced—such as 'work', 'works', 'worker', 'worked'—the limit of new words could be relaxed though not entirely omitted.

Every word, once introduced, must be repeated in the same lesson and later lessons. Here again, in the writer's opinion, each word must be repeated at least twenty times in the text. The first five repetitions should be bunched in the lesson in which the word appears for the first time; the rest of the fifteen repetitions could be spread over the succeeding lessons. Once more, it may not be possible to do so in the first few lessons, but the suggested number of repetitions should be achieved as soon as possible. The point is that the repetitions must sound natural and not strained and boring. This is where the dialogue method becomes useful. For example, in a lesson on the use of fertilizers, the words nitrogen, phosphorus (or phosphates) and potassium (or potash) may be new. They can be repeated in a dialogue in an interesting way, as in the following:

A. There are many things which the soil must have to give us good crops. But of these many things, three things are important.
B. Why are they more important than others?
A. They are more important than others because a crop takes them up in large quantities and, if we take crop after crop from our land, our land will soon have very little of them left in it to give us more good crops.
B. What are these three things?
A. They are nitrogen, phosphorus and potassium. Nitrogen, phosphorus and potassium are good for our crops and our crops take them up in large quantities, so that less and less of them are left for the new crops. What three things did I mention, as good for our crops?
B. Nitrogen, potassium and phosphorus.
A. Very good: nitrogen, phosphorus and potassium. Now, I will tell you why nitrogen is good for our crops, why potassium is good for our crops and why phosphorus is good for our crops.

We see here that the three new words—nitrogen, potassium and phosphorus—have been repeated, each five times, and it has been done in the more or less effortless way of talking naturally in a dialogue.

While we are talking of the dialogue style, we would like to mention that the characters between whom the dialogue takes place in the text should remain constant throughout the reading text. In the first place, it gives the text a genuine story form, which is an asset in teaching literacy to beginners. Second, the readers identify themselves with the persons in the dialogue. Identification with these characters would lead to an easier assimilation of the technical information given in the text.

Another interesting way of repeating words, naturally and with pedagogic advantage, is that of comparison, as shown in the following example:

A. Now look at the vines on C's land and the vines on D's land. D's vines are large because he has put fertilizers containing nitrogen on his land. But C has not put fertilizers containing nitrogen on his land, so his vines are not so large.

B.   Oh yes! I now see how nitrogen is good for our vines.

A.   Yes, nitrogen is good for vines. Now look at the bunches of grapes on the vines on D's land. They are large bunches containing big grapes. D has put fertilizers containing phosphorus and potassium on his land. C's bunches and his grapes are small, because he has not put fertilizers containing phosphorus and potassium.

B.   Yes. Now I see that, if we want our vines to give us good yield, we must give our land fertilizers containing nitrogen, potassium and phosphorus. Nitrogen will make our vines large; and phosphorus and potassium will make the clusters, and the grapes in the clusters, big.

A.   So you now understand why we should put fertilizers containing nitrogen, phosphorus and potassium on our land.

We see in the above that the words nitrogen, phosphorus and potassium have been repeated in the natural way of speaking—nitrogen seven times, phosphorus and potassium five times each—in a short passage.

Another important point to be kept in mind is the ratio of new words in a lesson to the number of words in the same lesson which are repeated from previous lessons. In the author's view this ratio should not be less than one new word to seventy or eighty repeated words in a lesson. Here, again, it is not possible to keep this ratio in the first ten to twelve lessons. But it should be kept in mind and an attempt should be made to reach this ratio as soon as possible. This will make the lessons easier and, therefore, pleasanter to read—an important element in the pedagogy of literacy.

The first spiral text may have a total of 170 to 220 words in 35 to 45 lessons, depending on the writer's over-all plan for dividing the literacy course into the first and second spirals and, of course, the nature of the subject matter. Of this total vocabulary, some words will be technical words, others will be the words common to the everyday speech of the participants. Technical words, of course, would occur with less frequency in the spoken language of the common population speaking that language. In tackling such technical words, we should try to use those words which have a high frequency status at least in the subject-matter context of literacy: those words should be used which people interested in the subject matter will use frequently in discussing their day-to-day concerns.

Use of illustrations

The reading materials for the literacy courses should be liberally scattered with illustrations. It is generally accepted that line-drawings can have a higher teaching value than light-and-shade pictures or photographs because in line-drawings we can manipulate the amount of information included.

The illustration should be placed near the text to be illustrated and should reinforce the message given in the text. This is the primary function of illustration in the reading materials for beginners. Second, the illustrations may also help to get the reader over the handicap of his reading vocabulary and illustrate ideas which his reading vocabulary cannot cope with. For example, in the reading text for factory workers, the present writer tried to put across in the sixth lesson the idea of keeping the factory floor clean by not throwing odds and ends on it. This was achieved, through the dialogue form, within a vocabulary of eight words, with the help of three line drawings on page 46.

The position of the illustration on a page is also an important point to be considered. If a small picture would be adequate for the purpose, it is best to put the text on one side of the page and the line-drawing, illustrating the text or supplementing it, level with it on the same page. In a language like English, which is read from left to right, it is better to put the picture on the right side of the page level with the line or lines it illustrates. In a language like Farsi, which is written from right to left, the line-drawing would come on the left side of the page. Further, where an illustration cannot be placed level with the text, it should immediately follow the text it illustrates and not be put before it. In cases where a sequence of processes is to be illustrated it would be best to put the illustrations, each illustration depicting one step in the process, in one line on a page, the sequence of illustrations going the same way as the language of the text.

What we have said here regarding the positioning of an illustration has been said with the pedagogical aspect in view. Some writers have mentioned the positioning of the illustrations in the text from the aesthetic point of view. But, in our view, the didactic positioning of an illustration is of paramount consideration in literacy teaching at this stage.

The text and the illustrations plus, in some cases, related charts make up a lesson in the reading text. Each lesson, unless it is in the nature of a summary of previous lessons, must bear on one topic and one topic alone. For the first few lessons, a line in the text should consist of only one short sentence. When a lesson and its illustrations attain a length which overflows a page, and when the sentences become so lengthy that they cannot be contained in one line, it will be necessary to divide the text into paragraphs. Each lesson will have its own title within the vocabulary range built by the end of the previous lesson and the new words in the present lesson. When a lesson goes into many paragraphs, it is best to break the monotony of the page by putting in topic headings immediately preceding the paragraph with which a new topic starts. This will also add to the comprehensibility of the text.

From: *My First Book in English* by Sohan Singh

Ben, No.

Not here.

Do not put it here.

Put it here.
Do put it here.

No Sam. Not here. Not here

Put it here, Ben.

If we regulate the dose of new words in every lesson in the reading text as explained above, the linguistic sequencing will almost be taken care of in the process. Almost, because, as we shall see later, the instructor's contribution to actualizing the learning of reading is by no means negligible. However, we must say a few words regarding the subject-matter sequencing of the reading text.

Our freedom to select the order of presentation of subject matter is limited at the beginning of a literacy course by the limitation of the sight vocabulary of learners. This limitation is especially restricting when we must adopt the chronological sequencing of the logical order. In such cases, the first ten to fifteen lessons represent the preparation for the subject matter. For example, in one case, where the writer prepared a first spiral reading materials on the cultivation of wheat, the chronological order starts with the preparation of the soil for sowing wheat. But, in view of the requirements of vocabulary, this could only be taken up after about twelve lessons. Nevertheless, these dozen or so lessons, too, had to deal with the subject matter. So we introduced two persons in dialogue with each other, one of whom teaches the other how to grow wheat to ensure a higher yield. The dialogue could be general and thus could handle vocabulary control better. It was only when a sight vocabulary of about sixty words had been built up that the technology of the wheat crop could be treated in the proper chronological order.

Similar problems will be met with in the logical order and similar solutions will have to be invented. It is logical that before an industrial worker starts his work on a machine, he must see that the machine is cleaned, oiled and the safety devices are put on. The logic of the subject, therefore, requires that cleaning and oiling of the machine, and use of safety devices should precede the working of the machine.

It will depend on the skill and imagination of an instructional materials writer to reconcile the two demands of ordering subject matter and ordering vocabulary. Lesson XXXIII reproduced overleaf from *My First Book of English* would indicate that, at the later stages of the first spiral, reconciling demands of subject matter and vocabulary is no longer too problematic. The instructions included in the *Teachers' Handbook* for presenting this lesson are also reprinted to demonstrate the inter-dependence between the student's book and the teacher's handbook. We must also remember that illustrations and the instructor's intervention are integral in the teaching of reading. There will be no difficulty in reconciling all these various demands if the instructor plays his part well.

LESSON XXXIII
USE THE RIGHT TOOL FOR A JOB

In the workshop it is all steel - steel and steel. Big steel and small steel.

A machine is made of steel. It is big steel. Small tools, like a chisel, a file and a hammer are made of steel. That is small steel. We have to have a machine made hard. We have to have all our tools made hard. And steel is hard. So all machines are made from steel and all tools are made from steel.

But the steel of a chisel is not the steel of a hammer, and the steel of a hammer is not the steel of a file.

The steel of a hammer is hard. But it is made hard for hammer work. The steel of a chisel is hard, but it is made hard to cut with. And so is the steel of a file hard, but it is made hard to do file work, that is to say, to cut small.

If you use a file like a hammer, that is not the right use of it. You will break the file. So will you break a chisel if you use it like a hammer, for that is not the right use of a chisel.

You break a chisel when you use it like a hammer, for the steel of a chisel is not made for hammer work. It is made to cut with. And you break a file when you use it like a hammer, for the steel of a file is not made for hammer work. It is so made that we can cut small with it.

So it is that we said that there is a right tool for a job. A file and a chisel can not do the job that a hammer can do. The job that a chisel can do a hammer and a file cannot do that. And a file can do the job that no hammer, no chisel can do.

Always use the right tool for a job. This is safety - safety not for you, but safety for your tool.

STEEL	steel	*steel*
MADE	made	*made*
CHISEL	chisel	*chisel*
FILE	file	*file*
HAMMER	hammer	*hammer*
HARD	hard	*hard*
USE	use	*use*
BREAK	break	*break*

LESSON XXXlll

1. You will remember that in Lesson XXV Sam had told
    Ben that there is a right tool for every job.
    Our story gives a reason why all tools cannot
    be used for all purposes.

    You find so much steel in a workshop. Big
    machines are all made of steel. Small but very
    useful things like nails, bolts and nuts and
    screws, all are made of steel. This is so
    because machine parts have to be hard, tools
    have to be hard and there is nothing so hard
    and less costly and easily available as steel.
    (Write down on the black board - steel and hard).

    All this is likely to give us the impression
    that all steel is the same. But no, there are
    many kinds of steel and many qualities of steel.
    Steels are made in different degrees of hardness.
    Some steel is very hard. It can cut other things,
    but when you use it for other purposes or when
    you strike it with a hammer it will break. They
    are so made (write on the black board made) by
    those who make steel in their workshops.

    Let us take three tools - a hammer, a chisel and
    a file. (Write down on the black board hammer,
    chisel, file). Even if you take a piece of steel
    from a hammer head and sharpen it, it will not be
    able to cut as well as a chisel does. But a
    hammer can stand heavy blows, while a chisel
    will break (write break on the black board)
    sometimes even with a light hammer blow. But a
    chisel can cut metal as a knife can cut card
    board. So that is the proper use of chisel.
    (Write use on the black board). Similarly, a
    file is made from a steel that can cut fine, and
    the proper use of a file is to file. So it is
    because of the different qualities of steel from
    which they are made that some tools are good for
    some purpose, while they are no good for other
    purposes. And when a tool-maker makes a tool, he
    makes it from that kind of steel, which is best
    for the purpose to which the tool will be put.

To put it to any other use will ruin the tool
and sometimes it may even break it.

Quite humorously the Lesson ends with these
words: This is safety – safety not for you, but for
your tools. Really, it is also for your safety.
For you remember we also read in this book that it
is unsafe to work with bad tools. And even if you
don't break a tool, you certainly make it a bad
tool for its right use, if you use it for a
purpose for which it was not made.

We will now read the story from our Book. But
before we do this please note these words we have
taken down on the black board. We never had so
many new words in a lesson. But many of them are
not really so new for us. We have met the words
hammer, chisel, file quite often in our
exercises. We have also come across the words
hard, steel, made, but and break. You will find them
all in your word book. The only really new word
is use. (Even if the seven words we have mentioned
come from the word book, spell and pronounce them
with the class, pointing out the vowel sounds.
Point out the new sound of u here, which is the
same as the name of the letter. Point out also
that the s in use, has the z sound, or the sound
it has in is.

Now proceed as in paragraph 3 of Lesson IX).

3.   a) Of the eight new words in this Lesson four are
quite simple. Steel has the vowel ee with its
long e-sound. Made has the a-e (a-dash-e) vowel
with its long a-sound. File has the i-e (i-dash-
e) vowel with the long i-sound. Hard has a as
in fast sound.

      b) We have also met break in our exercises. We
have so far met with three sounds of the
combined vowel letters ea. The most common ea
sound is that of long e, as in clean, easy, sea.
But we have also met with the short e sound of
ea, as in head, health, thread. In break it has
the long a sound as in make. There are only two

common English words where it has this sound –
break and great. Remember these two words, and
take them down in your word book.

c) Hammer and chisel are two syllable words –
ham-mer and chi-sel. In both the accent is on
the first syllable and so we have the short a
sound in hammer and the short i sound in chisel.
The e in both the second syllables is silent.
Note that the s in chisel again sounds like z.

d) The sound of u in use is a new vowel sound.
If you quickly sound first the short i-sound
and then the u sound as in put – i-u, you
will make this sound of u in use. We may call
it the long u sound – the sound which gives
the word its name – just as the long sounds of
a,e,i and o give the names to these letters.

The most common sound of u is its short sound
as in but. In common words the sound of u as
in put is more common, but in general, the
long u sound (as in use) is the more common.
Try to read these words in which u has this
long u-sound: human music duty beauty or
beautiful and the word we used to name a
tense – future. In future the first u has the
long u sound, while the second u has the short
u sound. Note that the syllable ture in future
sounds cher, where e is silent. Wherever you
find this syllable ture you sound it as cher.

4. You may take down duty and future in your word
book as examples of u-sound words.

5. (Practise with flash cards these words: steel
hammer chisel made file break hard use great
duty future fire).

6. (Now ask the students one by one to read the
sentences in Supplementary Reading 28).

7. (Ask the students to make their own sentences
with the words in paragraph 5 above. Note down
good sentences on the black board).

8. (The students may now proceed to their Workbook
Lesson XXXlll).

The instructor's role in actualizing reading

The instructor's role in bringing instructional materials to life, and thus in actualizing learning by adult readers, can be discussed in terms of the following tasks:

1. Making experience charts.
2. Revising and reinforcing the reading vocabulary and technical content of previous lessons.
3. Helping the participants to make a reading acquaintance with new words which will appear in the day's lesson.
4. Ensuring that the participants read with comprehension.
5. Helping the participants to improve their oral reading and to acquire the skill of silent reading.
6. Helping the participants to improve their reading speed.
7. Helping the participants to extend their reading vocabulary: first, by crossing over from words learnt to new words, and to families of words; and, second, by helping the participants to learn some special words of intrinsic interest to them.
8. Teaching the participants how to use a dictionary.
9. Helping the participants to read questions in their workbook.

Making experience charts

Experience charts are a few sentences written by the instructor on the blackboard on a topic of the day that has excited the interest of the participants. The topic may be the celebration of a festival, election of members to their co-operative society or union, political elections, or the visit of a V.I.P. to the area. It may thus be any unusual event that has excited people in the area. Sometimes it may be a folk song or folk tale relating to the emotion of the group on a particular day. The purpose is to sustain and to strengthen the motivation for learning reading and writing. Experience charts also help in the process of removing the psychological barriers between the speaking-listening mode of a language and its reading-writing mode.

The technique of constructing experience charts on the spur of the moment is to let the instructor and the participants together talk about the topic. As the discussion proceeds the instructor writes simple sentences on the blackboard in which some key words are repeated. These sentences are spoken by someone in the group and are written more or less as they are spoken, perhaps with slight modification to suit the structuring of an experience chart. Here is an example of an experience chart on the subject of Diwali—the widely celebrated 'festival of lights' in India:

Tomorrow is Diwali.
On Diwali our people have great fun.
On Diwali night our people light their homes.
On Diwali night children have great fun with fire-crackers.
And the elders have great fun to see their children having great fun with crackers.
Diwali is a great day for our people.
On Diwali our people wish a happy new year to their relatives and friends.

As the instructor writes on the blackboard he also speaks each word aloud. As a sentence is completed, he repeats it. At the end of the discussion—which should never be allowed to get insipid—he repeats each sentence slowly, pointing out to each word as it is spoken. He may then ask the participants what words they think are important and to note these words down—or maybe a sentence or two—in their notebooks. The instructors should have some experience in constructing experience charts as part of their training.

Revising words already learnt
It is important that the instructor should start his day's task by reviewing the previous day's lesson, from the point of view of both subject matter and literacy. Insofar as the linguistic content is concerned, he may write the words taken at random from the previous lesson or lessons on the blackboard or use flashcards and ask individual group members to say the words. Or he may ask individuals in the group to write them on the blackboard, which others may then read.

Writing and reading, coding and decoding, are so entwined with one another in the process of becoming a literate that the two must be taught together. We have treated the teaching of writing in a separate chapter merely as a teaching device. It is also very desirable to have a full revision lesson after every five to seven lessons wherein the whole of the technical and linguistic intake of the group is reviewed.

Teaching new words
This is done before the day's lesson is read by the participants and is done in two ways. First, the topic of the day's lesson is discussed point by point in the group. The instructor takes the lead by highlighting the various aspects of the problem. He fills in those important gaps which the group may have overlooked. In the course of this discussion the new words which are mentioned and which will also appear in the day's lesson are written down by the instructor on the blackboard. Each word is pronounced by the instructor as it is being written by him. The word is then spoken by group members.

Second, after the discussion and before the reading of the lesson starts, the instructor shows the flashcards for the new words in the day's lesson, mixed with flashcards of a few words from the previous lessons that may not have been mastered by some members of the group. When the instructor feels that the new words introduced will not prove much of an obstacle to the reading of the lesson, the reading of the lesson itself is taken up.

Reading with comprehension

Just as speaking a language is a sharing of minds, reading should also be a sharing of minds. Reading, which is a sharing of minds between the writer and the reader, is called reading with comprehension. Reading with comprehension is not only understanding the words in a sentence, it is also understanding what sorts of currents were going through the writers's mind when he wrote these words.

Take, for example, the sentence: 'He is a boy'. Depending on the context, the sentence may just be giving information that the person in question is a boy—and not a girl. Or, depending on the context, it may be a sneering reference to the boy, which may aptly be put into words as 'he is a mere boy'. The instructor can help learners understand these subtleties by asking questions, such as: 'What does the writer really mean by this—was he joking? was he annoyed?'.

Both to improve and to test comprehension, the instructor may ask the group members to read a sentence, or a paragraph, or the whole lesson, before he questions individual group members to locate and read the reply to his question from the text, or to answer his question orally.

Oral reading and silent reading

When a learner in reading starts on his task, the first few lessons will obviously be read by him in a loud voice so that the teacher can hear that he is reading correctly. It is often the case that the early lessons are read in a monotonous voice. Ultimately, oral reading should reproduce the cadence of the spoken language. And so, from the very beginning, the instructor should, by example and by persuasion, insist that a lesson, when orally read, sounds like ordinary speech, with its rhythm, intonation and appropriate facial expression. When the learner does so, the instructor knows that the reader is reading with comprehension and not merely wrestling with words.

As soon as possible, the learner must be brought to read silently. Some writers have suggested that silent reading should start from the very beginning of reading. I believe this is not possible and, didactically too, it is better that his first lessons should be read so that the instructor knows that the participant is recognizing words correctly. By the tenth to twelfth lesson, he will probably have picked up a sight vocabulary of which some words repeat quite often in the language he speaks. It is then time for the instructor to start the reader on silent reading. Even then, like the child that talks to himself when he is thinking, some of the readers will be found to read orally to themselves.

The instructor need not be in too desperate a hurry to stop them 'reading to themselves'. The first silent reading should tackle the reading material paragraph by paragraph. The instructor should ask the group to read the first paragraph of the lesson silently and give them reasonable time to read it with comprehension. After this, he may question individual participants to know how far they have been able to share the mind of the writer. From a paragraph read and digested silently, the instructor may go on to let the participants read a full page silently, questioning them later to find out if they have understood the contents of the page. Then, after about the twentieth lesson, he can ask the group to read an entire lesson silently and question them to find out if their silent reading has been reading with comprehension.

There are two ways in which the instructor can increase the reading speed of learners. We have spoken above of exposing to the participants flashcards which may have words (or even small phrases) written on them. One way of promoting reading speed is gradually to reduce the time of exposure of those flashcards, especially flashcards for words learnt in earlier lessons.

The second and more formal way to increase reading speed is to ask the reader to read a passage silently as quickly as possible, and to read it with comprehension. The instructor notes the time the learner has taken in reading through the passage. From this he calculates the time the reader takes in reading 100 words. This process is repeated—not on the same lesson, nor on the same day—and the reader is asked to compete with himself in reducing his reading time for 100 words. Every time the reader reads the passage indicated by the instructor, the latter asks him questions to see if the reader has read the passage with comprehension, for reading speed without comprehension has no meaning.

Reading with speed and comprehension presupposes silent reading and expert skipping. Skipping means going through a passage omitting to read certain portions of it to find an answer to a certain question. Skipping is possible only when a fairly large number of words and phrases have become sight words and sight phrases. One part of a sentence, usually its first part, gives a clue to the part omitted in rapid reading; and the reader has grasped the style of the author of the passage and the trend of argument so well that he feels he can find what he is seeking with a high degree of certainty, even if he were to omit a part of a sentence or whole sentences. This kind of rapid reading can come only when the reading ability of the reader has matured. A start can be made even in the later stages of the first spiral.

Extended reading vocabulary

There are three ways in which the literacy instructor can expand the participants' reading-writing vocabulary beyond their reading text. In the first place, he can take a new word appearing in the day's lesson and, with the help of words or letters learnt in earlier lessons, transform the new word into another word by changing, substituting, adding or taking away letters. To do this it is necessary that every time a new word appears in a lesson, it should be analysed into its constituent letters, the names of the letters and their shapes—there may be different shapes of the same, letter in different contexts, i.e. written, printed, capitals and small letters or in the beginning, middle and end of a word, as in the Arabic script.

There are four points to be noted in the transformation of words as suggested above. First, the participants must already have been acquainted with the letters which we manipulate in transmuting one word into another. Second, whenever a change is made in a word, the pronunciation of the new combination of letters must be called from the participants. Third, whenever a new word is formed from a word which has already been learnt by the group, the new word must be spoken in a sentence. When all the words in the sentence have already been learnt by the participants up to that time, the whole sentence containing the newly made word may be written down on the blackboard. Fourth, in transmuting a word into a new word, as far as possible, the new word should be one which the reader will meet with in later lessons. The participants should be asked to note down such words in their notebooks. It would be better if the participants are made to write meaningful sentences containing the new words.

The second way of expanding the participants' vocabulary is for the instructor to teach sight clues which go to make a family of words from a single word. These sight clues are the prefixes and suffixes which are a prominent structural feature of any language. Thus, from the words 'work', 'clean', 'move', etc., we can make the following words: 'worker', 'works', 'worked', 'working', etc.; 'cleaner', 'cleans', 'cleaned', 'cleaning', etc.; and 'mover', 'moves', 'moved', 'moving', etc. To take an example from Farsi, from the infinitive *Kun* (=do), with the help of simple and easily recognized inflections, a whole family of words can be conjured up: *Kunam* (I do), *Kuni* (you do), *Kunad* (he does), *Kuneem* (we do), *Kuned* (you all do), *Kunand* (they do).

A good deal of practice is needed for the participants to become so familiar with such inflections, suffixes and prefixes that, after the concept 'sight words', we can call them 'sight-inflections'. This practice should be given by the teacher in his classwork and also given through the workbook for participants. If this is done, the approximately 200 words that may form the sight words learnt by the participants in the first spiral of work can easily be expanded to 500 or more. This will enable them to take a leap from the stage of learning to read to the stage of reading to learn.

The third process of expanding the vocabulary of participants is for the instructor to teach them to write and read some very useful and emotionally positive words. Among these words the top claim belongs to the name of a participant. Some experts in reading have suggested that in an adult class the writing by every participant of his own name should be taught from the very first day of an adult literacy class. I must say that I am partial to this idea. Reading and, of course, writing by a participant of the name of his father, other members of his group, his village, the instructor's name and such other personal words would follow immediately. The names of days and months and years, and the writing of dates must also follow. The instructor can even invite the participants to suggest words which they would love to read and write. Here again, we see that reading and writing cannot be separated, one from the other.

Using the dictionary

If we stick to our objectives for the first spiral—that it should carry the learner from learning to read to reading to learn—it is essential that the instructor should initiate the participants in the use of a dictionary in the latter stages of the first spiral itself. The skill of using a dictionary is based on the order of the alphabet in a language; learning this order must start not later than the middle of the first spiral. When this order has been learnt, the participants should be asked to locate the words they know so far in the dictionary. From this they can go on to read the meaning or meanings of the word.

In the final stages of the first spiral, the participants should be asked to find out from the dictionary the meaning of a new word in the new lesson. If the word carries more meanings than one, they should be asked to choose the meaning that fits the word in the context in which it appears in the lesson. The learner can even be initiated into looking for the roots of words and shown how a whole family of words springs from this root, such as 'duct', 'abduct', 'induct', 'conduct', 'deduct', etc. This insight can help the reader to guess at the meaning of a word and thus to expand his vocabulary.

The need for learning to use a dictionary at a certain point in a literacy course is of such importance that it is a pity most languages do not have a dictionary which could be used in elementary literacy classes. What we need in literacy classes is not *The concise Oxford dictionary,* but a small dictionary listing about six to seven thousand words, like one of the simpler dictionaries compiled by Thorndike.

Using a workbook

A participant must know what kind of work he has to do in a certain lesson in his workbook, corresponding to a lesson in his reading text. This he cannot do in the early stages because, due to his lack of reading vocabulary, he cannot read the questions in the workbook.

It is, therefore, one of the tasks of the instructor to initiate his group into understanding what task the various exercises in the workbook require of the group. This he can do in two ways. In the first place, he can show them the structure of an exercise, say, in the first lesson in the workbook, and then ask them to find out similar exercises in the following lessons. For example, one of the exercises in the workbook may be to underline a required word from among a number of words. A good workbook will maintain an identical structure for this type of exercise in later lessons. This will make it easier for the participants to do this exercise. However, this is not so much reading as pre-reading.

The instructor will also teach his group members to read certain key words in certain types of exercises. For example, many exercises will require the participants to fill in the blanks in the material that follows, and the teacher should set aside a time to teach the keywords of this type of exercise, for example, 'fill' and 'blanks'. If the instructor does his job well, a participant will become independent on how the various types of exercises in the workbook must be tackled.

Summary

Five principles of the pedagogy of literacy instruction are stated as a background to the discussion of teaching reading in the first spiral. They are: (a) establishing relationships between the two modes of using symbols in speech and in reading; (b) establishing reading-writing responses in the learner; (c) maximizing the learner's absorption of stimuli, that is, printed words and phrases; (d) appropriate alteration between practice and rest periods; and (e) imposing a rhythm on the pattern of work in groups.

Detailed discussion follows on the construction of a text for the teaching of reading in the first spiral, covering questions of word doses, teaching sight words and phrases, approaches to presentation, and use of illustrations. The role of the instructor is emphasized in bringing instructional materials to life and to actualizing the learning of reading by learners. The tasks to be undertaken by instructors, to increase the reading competence of learners and to take them towards fast and silent reading with comprehension, are elaborated.

CHAPTER FIVE

Teaching writing in the first spiral

It is impossible to place the teaching of reading and writing in separate water-tight compartments. In fact, if we take the recognition of words as the basic learning technique of literacy, writing of words is the best way of making words recognizable. Hence, the day that a person starts to learn reading is the same day for starting to learn writing. In the following we will give some practical ideas on the teaching of writing. We will take a broader view of writing; making a diagram or making a chart will also be seen as exercises in writing.

For learning writing, the learner must have the following minimum equipment—paper or a slate for writing words or taking dictation from the instructor, a notebook in which to write words and sentences, or to draw diagrams and charts of more lasting importance and, of course, the workbook which includes exercises for the teaching of writing.

The concept of 'kinaesthetic words'

Just as a word is the basic unit of learning to read, so too is a word the basic unit of learning to write. But, whereas the secret of learning to read is to make some basic words into sight words, the secret of learning to write is to make some basic words into 'kinaesthetic words'. However, there is this difference between sight and kinaesthesia: while the eye moves in junps and pauses in reading, the kinaesthetics of writing require a continuous movement of the hand.

Learning to write also implies an anlysis of words into a sequence of letters and then writing each letter in the proper sequence to remake the whole word. We learn to write the letters—maybe the same letters in different shapes for languages like Farsi and Urdu. But it is only when we have practised writing a whole word that we form a kinaesthetic image of the word. Thus, we learn to write letters in the context of writing meaningful words, and even meaningful sentences.

Steps in learning to write

The first words a beginner learns to write will, of course, be those that he will be copying from the blackboard. He will be copying the movement of the instructor's hand as he writes words on the blackboard. He will imitate those movements and internalize them. The instructor, therefore, must write every word slowly so that the participants can watch the continuous movement of the instructor's hand in writing those words. The participants then carefully copy the writing of each word on their slates (or wooden plates).

After copying the words as written by the instructor, the participants will, as an exercise in their workbooks, copy the same words as they are printed. The next step is to write the same words as they are dictated by the instructor. The fourth step will be correcting the words which the participants may have misspelt or formed badly. In the fifth step the participants will be required to write the words they have learnt in a 'fill in the blanks' exercise, where the context requires one of the words learnt to be written in the blank space. Finally, in his dictation, the instructor may require the participants to write unseen words created from words and letters within words already learnt. Instructions for conducting these six stages in the teaching of writing words should be put in the instructor's guide.

The instructor's guide should also include two other points on which the participants can be assisted. First, the words as written by the participants should be legible. This means that the letters composing the words should be well formed and in the correct sequence. Second, the illiterate adult who comes to the literacy class is usually habituated to the use of movements of large muscles, so that he writes the words in large letters. He has to be helped to use small-muscle movements in writing, so that he can form words in writing of small size.

Just as it requires reading a word many times before it becomes a sight word for the reader, similarly, it requires a word to be written a number of times before it becomes a kinaesthetic word for the writer—a kinaesthetic unity. There should be a place for such writing in the group sessions, as well as in the workbook.

From the basic writing of words, the instructor should go on to teach the beginner words of personal importance. The writing of his own name, his father's name, his friends' names, the name of his village, the days of the week, the date, the months of the year, and the year itself, should be taught. The writing of a participant's name may start, if not with the first session of the group, then as soon as possible.

About the fifth lesson, it would be time to require the participant to start writing whole sentences. At first, these will be small, simple sentences. For example, the instructor (or the workbook) may require the participant to write the answer to a question as given in the reading text, or to write the question for an answer which is already provided. When, with a growing reading vocabulary, the technical instruction given in a lesson becomes more detailed, the participant's workbook may require him to write a number of sentences in a sequence.

In the last stages of the first spiral, the participant may be asked by the instructor to write a short summary of the lesson. The instructor should check the participant's writings to make sure that: (a) the grammar of the language is not violated; (b) the punctuation, where necessary, is provided; (c) the lines are written straight and not sloping, as is usually the case with beginners in writing; and (d) of course, the content of the sentences is correct from the point of view of the subject matter.

Some subjects require diagrams or charts to be drawn by the learner. Usually, instructions for making these charts and diagrams would have been provided in the reading text or by the instructor. The instructor has to check the correctness of the contents of the charts or the diagrams and also, where needed, the scale. For example, near the end of a reader on, say, the growing of wheat, the participants may be asked to make a chart of the calendar of the crop—when is the land prepared, when is the seed sown, when is the first irrigation given, etc. Or a housewife may be required to make out a chart for feeding a baby of, say, eighteen months. On one side, she will give the times when the baby is to be fed; on the other side, the food to be given. The point in all this is that charts and diagrams are encoding devices to be decoded later. Making charts and diagrams is, therefore, also a form of writing.

We mentioned in the previous chapter that the speed of reading is a sign of maturity of the reader. So also, speed in writing is a sign of the learner's mastery of the art of writing. A workbook, because of its very nature, cannot teach writing speed and, hence, it will be a task for the instructor to do so. We have seen that dictation by the instructor is part of a unit lesson. The instructor can gradually increase the speed with which he dictates or, when participants are required to write answers to a question, a time limit may be set for this work.

Finally, the instructor and the workbook between them may have to induce the participants to practise different types of writing. We have already mentioned drawing of charts and diagrams. Other forms of writing, depending on the subject matter of the literacy class, may be: drawing up household accounts; instructions for preparing food for a baby; writing a popular poem; writing tit-bits, etc. A large part of such forms of writing may be left to the second spiral, but a beginning can be made in the first spiral itself.

Summary

Some ideas are presented in this chapter on the teaching of writing to adult learners. Parallel to the concept of 'sight words' in reading, the concept of 'kinaesthetic words' in writing is presented. Some practical hints are provided to the instructor for teaching writing to adult learners. Six steps in learning to write are suggested as follows: (a) copying words written by the instructor on the blackboard; (b) copying words or letters in the workbook; (c) writing words dictated by the instructor; (d) correcting misspelt words; (e) filling in blanks by writing single words in sentences as part of the exercises in the workbook; and (f) writing words and sentences of significance to the participants.

CHAPTER SIX

Workbook and instructor's guide: tools for integrated teaching of reading, writing and subject matter

The approach to literacy instruction proposed in this monograph assumes an underlying system. It assumes interdependence among teacher, learner and instructional materials; and integration of many different instructional processes. For instance, teaching of reading is integrated with the teaching of writing; and the teaching of these both is integrated, as far as possible, with the teaching of arithmetic. The teaching of the three Rs is integrated with the teaching of subject matter. There is an interdependence between the learner role and the teacher role. The teacher-learner relationship is dependent on suitably designed instructional materials that serve both the teacher and the learner. Finally, there is an interdependence between the two phases of becoming an independent reader—'learning to read' and 'reading to learn'.

This chapter focuses on the workbook and the instructor's guide, which are considered to be important elements of the total system of literacy instruction. Together they do some significant things for the programme. We have already referred to the usefulness of imposing a rhythm on the patterns of work of adults in literacy groups. Rhythm is an important element in the workbook, which sets the pattern of a participant's work on his own; and in the instructor's guide which sets the pace and pattern of work during a group session. Rhythm in both these items of instructional materials sets the order in which the various tasks should be done. It sets up an expectation of sequence in the participants' minds and, thus, contributes to a sense of security in them. That is an essential element of a desirable teacher-learner situation. The workbook and the instructor's guide carry within them a part of the integration process. They also pre-structure, in part, the instructional process and thereby assist teachers and learners in classes to maintain a certain level of performance. Thus, they make up for the typically brief training periods that literacy instructors go through before they start teaching.

Workbook

The workbook is an instructional tool of significance. We have already referred to its ability to pre-structure somewhat the instructional process, to integrate the three Rs and the subject matter, and to become the teacher's helping hand. Additionally, the workbook provides a record of the learner's progress. Both learners and instructor can look back on what has been learnt and how well. An examination of the workbooks in a class, or a whole literacy programme, can provide important feedback on the general suitability of instructional materials, training of instructors, and on teaching processes in the classrooms.

The workbook is essentially meant to test a participant's recognition of words and letters; to give him practice in writing and, thereby, also to test his comprehension of words, phrases and sentences, and to judge his grasp of the subject matter. There is hardly any difference between comprehending a piece of writing and grasping the subject-matter content of it. In the specimen exercises given in the following pages we would not, therefore, distinguish between those two objectives.

Six points relating to the make up and use of a workbook can be made. First, after every question, the workbook should provide a space for writing or marking a reply. Second, a rhythm should be preserved in each workbook lesson, that is, similar questions in different lessons should appear in the same order. For instance, linguistic questions relating to word recognition and writing of words may always come first, followed by subject-matter questions which, again, may be followed by miscellaneous exercises such as writing of name, date, names of months and days, etc. Third, a workbook should have a revision lesson after every five to seven lessons. The instructor and the participants will thus have the opportunity to review and consolidate the linguistic and subject-matter learning in the previous five to seven lessons. Fourth, a lesson in a workbook should be carried out immediately after the corresponding lesson in the reading text is finished. Fifth, before the participants start on a workbook lesson, the instructor must make sure that the participants know what is to be done in each exercise. If the rhythm of exercises is maintained, and if certain key words are taught to the participants, it will not present much of a problem to them to understand what is to be done in an exercise. Even where the instructor has to teach how an exercise is to be done, he should only indicate how that *type* of exercise is to be done and not do the exercise itself. Sixth, the exercises completed by the participants should be examined by the instructor as soon as possible and necessary guidance provided to the whole group or to some of the participants as appropriate.

Exercises for teaching recognition and writing of words
Insofar as the recognition of words is concerned, it may be helped by an exercise as follows:

Underline the word <u>Ben</u> in all its forms:

   Sam   Man   Ben   NEB   BEN   ben   SAM   BNE

It will be noticed that, in the wording of the exercise itself, the word Ben is underlined. This is meant to give a clue to the new learner that, in this type of exercise, he is expected to underline all such words from among the words which follow in whatever form—whether all letters capitalized, or only the first letter capitalized or all letters in the lower case.

A simple exercise requiring the writing of words can follow as in the following example:

Write on the blank lines the following words:
   This is Sam   This is Ben

   ....

   ....

   ....

   ....

   ....

It may be mentioned that though 'This is Sam' and 'This is Ben' are sentences, the exercise is really an exercise in copying words.

Participants can then move on to exercises which help in word recognition through writing the word and not through copying them. These exercises may require the participants to write the correct word under a picture, to correct a misspelt word or to fill in a blank in a sentence by writing the appropriate word in the blank space. Examples are:

Under each picture write the word which tells what it is:

   (Picture of   *(Picture of*   *(Picture of*   *(Picture of*
       Sam)   *Ben)*   *a man)*   *three men)*

In each of the three sentences, one word is written incorrectly. Write the word correctly on the line after the sentence:

This is his pen ....

This is his hend ....

Sem is a good man ....

Another variation of this exercise could be the following:

These words are incorrect. Write the words correctly under each incorrect word:
Thes   sam   putt   hend   gud

An exercise requiring a higher degree of mastery of words may use the technique of filling in the blanks. We may pick up a sentence from the reading text, drawing a one-word blank as follows:

Fill in the blanks in the following sentences:
Do not .... it here.
Ben, put it ....

The instructor's guide should suggest when these various exercises might be tackled by an adult group.

Another device inviting the participants to write words on their own asks them to write one or more words which rhyme with a given word or have a meaning opposite to the given word as indicated in the following two examples:

After each word write a word which rhymes with it:
do ....   life.........
will ....   air ....

After each word write a word with the opposite meaning:
good.......   thin ....
wet ....   right.......

We have seen that perfect control over the writing of a word necessarily requires the ability to write the letters and to write them in different shapes if the script of a language so requires. For recognizing and writing the letters the workbook should also contain the following types of exercise:

In the following after the letter given, write the same letter ten times:
B ....
b ....

Write the letters b or e under b or e in the following:
The boy saw Bob Kennedy in a bath of blood. Somebody had hurt him badly.

Against each of the letters given below write capital letters if the given letter is small, and write small letters if the given letter is capital:
A ...   P ...   H ...
e ...   u ...   B ...

Some letters are missing in these words. Fill the right letter in the blank:
Th...s is S...m
N...t her...
Pu... it h...re B...n

As mentioned earlier, a workbook should have a revision lesson after every five to seven lessons. Until the entire alphabet has been well learnt, it would be desirable to have an exercise giving the whole alphabet in its proper order in revision lessons and to ask the participants to circle (or underline or cross out) the letters already learnt.

One type of exercise which combines the learning of letters and words is as follows:

After each letter, write on the line a word which contains the letter you have learnt—in any form:
A.........   H.........   O.........   V ....
B.........   I ....   P.........   W.........

We have said that when a language has a simple dictionary the participants must be introduced to its use. The following types of exercise will be necessary for this purpose:

Arrange the following words in alphabetical order on the line given below them:
out file maker fine ours push easy pull
....

Look up the word 'machinery' in the dictionary and write the answers to these questions:
1. On what page of the dictionary do you find the word?...............................
2. What is the first meaning of the word as given in the dictionary?.....................

Exercises for teaching prefixes, suffixes and inflections
Whenever a word appears in the reading text in different persons and tenses, the instructor should teach the participants how the words are inflected or an auxiliary word brought in to express different persons and tenses. The workbook should help the instructor by including exercises such as the following:

Fill in the blanks in the following in accordance with the first line:

I do	You do	He does	We do	You do	They do
....	....	He cleans	....	....	....
I work	....	....	....	....	....
....	You keep	....	....	....	....

As new verbs are introduced in the text, the table can be enlarged. It is better to keep some old examples for the sake of revision.

Fill in the blanks as in the first line:

I do	I did	I will do	He does	He did	He will do
....	....	.......sleep	....	....	....
....	....	....	....	...kept	....
....	...worked	....	....	....	....
you do	you did	you will do			
....	....	....			
....	....	....			
....	....	....			

All the important inflexions, suffixes and prefixes in a language should be introduced by the instructor in his class and followed up as exercises in the corresponding lessons in the workbook. For example, take the suffix 'er' in English. The exercise in the workbook may run as follows:

Fill in the blanks as in the first line:

A man who works is called a   *worker.*

A man who cleans is called a   ....

The machine which extinguishes
a fire is called an   ....

Or to take an example from Farsi:

Write as one word:

mai+gir=	maigir
mai+pasham=	....
bah+gir=	bahgir
bah+pasham=	....
nah+gir=	nahgir
nah+pasham=	....

Comprehension of sentences and subject matter
Exercises in the workbook to check comprehension of sentences will be more or less similar to exercises to check word recognition. Here are a few examples:

Match the sentences and the pictures by drawing a line from the sentence to the picture:

Pick up this tool.	(*A picture of two men of equal height standing shoulder to shoulder.*)
The hammer head was loose.	(*A scene of falling rain.*)
I am as tall as you.	(*Picture of a saw.*)
You can cut wood with this tool.	(*Two men standing near a work table with a hammer on the ground— one man pointing the hammer to the other man.*)
It is raining.	(*A man working with a hammer— the hammer head flying from the handle.*)

Write the correct sentence on the line; the incorrect sentence is given above the line:

Will I do this.

....

I seed you yesterday.

....

Friend my, we go must.

....

What I can do today, I can do yesterday.

....

Fill in the blanks:

In what type of soil is the yield.........and in what type of.........is the yield less.

The yield from the Mexipak seed of wheat is much.........than the.........from the seed of local wheat.

Put the correct punctuation marks in the following:

Hasan said I will now tell you how to make red raisins
Tomorrow I will tell you how to make green raisins
Do you agree we should do that

Asad asks this question in the lesson: What kind of seed gives the highest yield? Write on this line the answer as it was given by Hasan:

....

We will now give some examples of exercises which will enable the teacher to check whether a participant has understood the subject-matter content of a lesson. There are six types of exercises that may be used in a workbook to achieve this purpose.

1. A question may be asked which needs an answer in one or two sentences, for example: What kind of seed gives the highest yield of wheat per hectare? The instructor should advise the participants to give their answer in complete sentences. For example, the desirable answer to this question is not to say 'Mexipak seed', but: 'Mexipak seed gives the highest yield of wheat per hectare'.

2. Multiple-choice questions provide another format for exercises. The participants may be asked to check the correct answer.

> To keep your teeth in a good condition, you should:
> Eat good food.
> Clean your teeth once a day.
> Clean your teeth after every meal.
> Chew tobacco.

It is generally agreed that in a multiple-choice question at least four alternatives should be given. More than four alternatives will only encumber the question. However, when more than one answer is correct the number of alternatives could be increased, as in the following:

> In order to obtain higher yields of wheat from your land, it is necessary that:
> You should sow local seed.
> Land should be ploughed once before sowing the seed.
> Land should be ploughed more than once.
> Land should be ploughed crosswise.
> You should sow Mexipak seed.
> Land should be ploughed deeply.
> Land should be cloddy.
> Put this mark—X—before the alternatives which are correct.

3. 'True or false', 'Yes or no' questions can also be used.

> Write Yes or No (or True or False) after the following sentences:
> Roughage is a necessary part of a good diet. ....
> Smoking is good for your throat. ....
> We should sleep not less than twelve hours a day. ....
> We must take plenty of water in a day. ....
> We should take a balanced diet. ....
> A balanced diet consists of bread, pickles and water. ....

4. In an earlier exercise we suggested matching pictures with their descriptions. Matching can be used in other settings also.

Draw a line from the name of a chemical fertilizer to the right quantity in which it should be mixed in the soil over one jarib of land:[1]

Diammonium phosphate   50 grams
                            30 kilograms
                            22 kilograms
                            28 kilograms
                            50 kilograms
        Urea   14 kilograms

5. In the latter part of the first spiral the instructor should start teaching the participants to make outlines or summaries of the lessons they have read. This activity will, of course, be carried on into the second spiral. The instructor should limit the number of sentences or words to be used in a summary; space for a summary should be provided in the workbook.

6. Exercises may also require the participants to make charts and drawings. The following types of exercises may be useful:

Make a scale drawing of your kitchen garden where you plan to raise cauliflowers. Show in the drawings the places where you will plant cauliflower seedlings, giving the number of seedlings you will plant.

Make a time chart of the operations involved in raising a wheat crop, giving the cost of each operation.

Instructor's guide

An instructor's guide should include both general guidelines for the instructors to follow as they conduct the programme, and specific points on how to conduct each particular lesson. There is a practical problem here. Our experience is that instructors do not always go through the material providing guidance for conducting each lesson. It is a task for them and it is not too much of a burden on their conscience to overlook reading it. Yet, through reasons of background, experience or training, instructors in literacy classes are not always able to do justice to their work if they do not read the instructions. An instructor's guide must, therefore, remain an essential part of the total instructional materials kit.

The general guidelines in an instructor's guide should be of two types. First, the instructor's guide should give the major guidelines for keeping good human relations in the adult literacy group they are leading. Most literacy instructors come from primary or lower secondary schools and

[1] A jarib measures 44 metres by 44 metres and is the basic unit of land measurement in Afghanistan.

they transfer their attitude towards schoolchildren to the adults in the literacy classes. The instructor's guide must caution the instructor against this. Also, the cultural traditions in the countries of low literacy promote a stereotype of teacher-pupil relations which put the learner in an inferior position. The result of these two factors is that, if the instructors do not relate with the adults as they should, the adults will keep away from their classes.

The second general type of instructions in the instructor's guide should give some hints on introducing learning materials to adults. If the reading text is in the dialogue form, as we have recommended, the instructor should introduce the characters to the learners. He should indicate what they will be talking about, how the illustrations will help in understanding the subject matter, and the necessity of doing related exercises in the workbook, etc.

A suggested rhythm for daily work

The rhythm, which we have already mentioned in Chapter IV, is brought out best in the instructor's guide. Different instructional material specialists may have somewhat different ideas about it. The following type of rhythm has been found to work well in literacy programmes with which this writer has been associated.

1. The first few minutes of class time may be spent on courtesies and pleasantries. If there has recently been a happening in the village or in the area, which has excited the interest of the people, some discussion may be started on it in the group and an experience chart made from the discussion. At the end of the discussion, the participants may select, and note in their notebooks, some interesting word or words that may have come out of the discussion.

2. A review of the previous lesson may follow. A participant may be asked to give very briefly the main points in the subject of the previous lesson. If some important point is left out by him, another participant may be asked to supplement him. Another participant may mention the new words that were learnt in the last session.

3. After the review comes the time for pre-reading discussion on the subject matter of the new lesson to be conducted that day. The instructor asks the class how much they already know on the subject and then supplements the discussion by bringing out important points not mentioned by participants. This is also the point in time when the instructor may introduce actual specimens, illustrations, charts and other audio-visual aids to the group. Of course, this can happen only if the

instructor has prepared himself by going through the lesson beforehand; and the instructor's guide has helped him to prepare for it. As the discussion proceeds, the instructor writes down on the blackboard the words that are used in the discussion and which will also occur in the new lesson. He does it slowly, simultaneously pronouncing the words.

4. At the close of the discussion, the instructor shows the flashcards for the new words in the day's lesson and asks the participants individually to say the word on each flashcard. He may also mix these with some other flashcards for difficult words from an earlier lesson. During the first few lessons, the participants should be allowed sufficient time to recognize the words by comparing them with the words written on the blackboard. Gradually, the time of the exposure of flashcards is reduced. (Before showing the flashcards the words on the blackboard should be erased.) The instructor should continue to show the flashcards until the new words are recognized at sight by most participants. But, the showing of flashcards should be stopped when the participants start getting bored with it.

5. The participants should then start reading the lesson. In the earlier lessons, when they are reading aloud, portions of the text may be read by various participants. In this way the text of the lesson may be read two or three times. When the participants start reading silently—around the tenth lesson or so—all of them read the lesson simultaneously.

6. In order to assist the instructor, the portion of the instructor's guide for the day's lesson should include questions for the instructor to test the participants' comprehension of what is read. The participants may be asked, individually and by turn, to answer the question or read the answer from the text. After about five or so lessons of silent reading, the participants may first read silently the whole lesson or some portion of it to answer the instructor's question and, while they are giving an oral reply to the question, they may indicate to the instructor and to others in the group the paragraph which includes the answer.

7. After the lesson has been read and after the details in the lesson have been grasped by the participants reasonably well, the instructor takes up the new words to anlyse them into their constituent letters. Any new letter which comes up in this analysis is then written on the blackboard in the various forms in which it appears in the printed and written language. New words are then constructed from letters and words already learnt. As far as possible, the instructor arrives at a new word by taking up a word already learnt and alters it by omitting letters, by changing the position of a letter or a combination of letters, or by putting a new letter or letters at the beginning or middle or end.

8. The instructor may then dictate sentences or isolated words. Dictation requires that the learner not merely reproduce words after the models of those words available on a page, but from models in the learner's mind. The dictation, of course, will cover the new words in the lesson and words learnt in previous lessons, and also words constructed through the analysis and synthesis of words referred to above.

9. In this part of the rhythm of a lesson, the instructor teaches the participants the writing of useful words mentioned earlier in this chapter, such as writing of personal names (of self, father, friends), names of days and months, writing dates and, if the subject matter requires, writing of accounts, records, etc.

10. The instructor introduces to participants the corresponding lesson in the workbook, clearing the hurdles that may arise from the participants' limited reading vocabulary.

11. Finally, it should be mentioned here that, just as a workbook has revision lessons after every five to seven lessons, so also an instructor's guide should have corresponding revision lessons in which instructors are given guidance on conducting reviews. A revision lesson in the instructor's guide will review the words learnt in the previous lessons, the letters of the alphabet learnt so far, inflections, suffixes and prefixes that were used in generating word families, and the technical knowledge acquired in the lessons being reviewed.

Summary

In this chapter we have discussed the role of the workbook and the instructor's guide within the total system of literacy instruction. The various instructional elements and the particular types of exercises to be included in these two items of instructional materials are delineated. The instructor's role in the use of these materials is also clarified.

CHAPTER SEVEN

Teaching arithmetic in the first spiral

Literacy, as we have suggested earlier, involves the mastering of reading and writing of two language systems—the language of words and the language of numbers. We have indicated also that these two language systems—the symbol system built upon words and the symbol system built upon numbers—have each been built on a logic of their own. The internal logic of each of these two systems must be followed in their teaching.

The problems of integrating arithmetic with reading and writing, on the one hand, and with the subject-matter content, on the other, have been referred to repeatedly. They are, indeed, difficult and raise several issues. The teaching of arithmetic to adult learners is a subject that merits separate and systematic attention. A brief discussion of the subject must, however, be included in the present monograph for the following reasons. We wish to state our commitment to the idea that learning numeracy is an important part of becoming literate. Not to include a chapter on the teaching of arithmetic in this monograph would be to sound less than convincing in our argument. Also, we have talked a lot about integrated teaching throughout this book. We wish to demonstrate that the instructor's guide and the workbook can be excellent tools for achieving this.

Numbers are indeed a language system. Arithmetic, as an expression of this language, has its own words and sentences. These are different from the words and sentences of everyday life, but they can be translated into the language of everyday life. For example, $3+5=8$, $3+6\neq8$, $8>5$, or $5<8$ are as good sentences as: 'John is a tall man'. They can be decoded into the spoken language, just as a written sentence in an alphabetical code can be translated into the spoken language. For example, $3+5=8$, is a sentence which when translated into everyday language would be: when five is added to three, we get eight. The sentence, $3+6\neq8$, can be read: six added to three does not make eight; $8>5$, can read: eight is greater than five; $5<8$ can read: five is less than eight.

Almost every adult knows how to count small numbers. Counting up to ten is not at all difficult, because our ten fingers help us this far. But counting large numbers becomes a problem for the illiterate. A farmer has to weigh his produce before he sells it; a housewife has to balance her family budget, or buy particular lengths of cloth and make money transactions. A modern farmer has to mix particular ratios of fertilizers and apply them to particular areas of the field. Most illiterates become lost when they start counting, adding, subtracting, multiplying and dividing big numbers. Fractions and decimals complicate the problem even more. Hence, teaching the language of arithmetic—and simple geometry— becomes a must in a literacy course.

The teaching of arithmetic (and simple geometry) in a literacy class requires three types of materials: an instructional guide for instructors; a workbook for participants in literacy groups; and a set of flashcards for practising basic facts in computation.

The instructor's guide is meant to give guidance to instructors on the basic skills which should be imparted to participants; how to impart them; and how to use these skills in solving the computational problems the participants will come across in their daily lives. The instructor's guide also gives the 'why' of arithmetical operations to be passed on to the participants, because teaching them merely the algorithms of computation would take away the educational base of teaching computation.

The workbook provides the participants with exercises which strengthen their skills in computation and problem solving. Just as some words must be made into sight words and kinaesthetic words if a learner has to achieve some degree of competence in reading and writing, so also some basic arithmetical facts have to be recognized at sight if the participants are to achieve facility in solving their computational problems.

Flashcards help the instructor to implant these basic skills in the minds of the participants.

The main themes and skills in computation that a literacy class needs to learn are as follows: (a) counting and place values; (b) addition, subtraction, multiplication and division—the four main arithmetical operations; (c) fractions and decimals; (d) proportions; and (e) some everyday measurements of lengths, weights and time.

In teaching these themes and skills a literacy instructor has to make the participants understand the principles underlying the arithmetical relations, if necessary with the help of diagrams, and to demonstrate their applicability in solving the participants' everyday problems. We will take these various topics one by one in the following paragraphs to illustrate the function of the instructor's guide and the workbook in imparting the themes and skills to the participants.

Counting and place values

Almost every adult understands the cardinal numbers—one, two, three, etc. Adults also know the ordinal nature of numbers—first, second, third, etc. Most adults can also count to ten, some to twenty or more. What they do not always know is how to read and write numbers in the form of numerals or in words. This can be easily taught by means of flashcards, with numerals on one side and the corresponding words on the reverse.

More importantly, neither adult participants in literacy classes nor, sometimes, their instructors, understand the magic of numbers and how that magic works. For example, there is no end to numbers. However big a number you may imagine, there is always a number which will be one more than it. Now, if each number had to have a name to indicate before which number it came and which number it followed, there would have to be infinite names because there are infinite numbers. It would be impossible to remember all those names! We know, of course, that we can write all kinds of numbers by merely using 0, 1, 2, 3, 4, 5, 6, 7, 8 and 9. This is possible because these numerals can have different place values.

We have said that while a literacy instructor may know his arithmetic quite well, he may not always be able to teach the concepts underlying arithmetical operations and, therefore, the instructor's guide must include detailed instructions on the teaching of the concepts of groupings of ten (ten; ten tens=hundred; ten hundreds=thousand; ten thousands=ten thousand; and so on) and of place values.

The instructor can make the idea of groupings and higher groupings, and of place values clear by using the following example:

/////////
These are nine sticks. These can be arithmetically written as 9.

(/////////)
This is one complete group of ten sticks. This is *one* group of ten (we use the symbol 1), and no other stick (we use the symbol 0). These sticks can be arithmetically written as 10.

(//////////)
(/////////)
These are two complete groups of ten sticks and three other sticks. There are two groups of ten (we use the symbol 2) and three other sticks (we use the symbol 3). These sticks can be arithmetically written as 23.

///

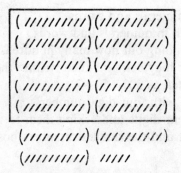

These are one big group of ten tens, three groups of ten, and five other sticks. There is one group of hundred (we use the symbol 1), three groups of tens (we use the symbol 3), and five other sticks (we use the symbol 5). These sticks can be arithmetically represented as 135.

Higher and higher groupings of ten can be built (ten hundreds, ten thousands, and so on) to write higher and higher numbers by assigning correspondingly higher and higher place values to the same numerals: 0, 1, 2, 3, 4, 5, 6, 7, 8 and 9.

A chart like the one given in Table 1 could also be included in the instructor's guide and used by the instructor to teach and explain both these concepts of groups of ten and of place values.

TABLE 1. *A chart explaining groups of ten and place values*

Hundred thousands	Ten thousands	Thousands	Hundreds	Tens	Units
				5	1
		4	5	3	8
	1	5	0	3	9

The role of the workbook at this stage would be: (a) to assist the instructor in teaching the concept of numbers, and reading and writing them in the form of numerals and words; and (b) to provide participants with the required practice. The following types of exercise may be useful:

1. Writing numbers 1 to 10, both in numerals and words. (The workbook may include illustrations of human fingers, which are universally used in counting small numbers, or of other familiar and significant objects to establish relationships between numbers and quantities.)
2. Writing of numbers 10, 20, 30, ... 90, both in the forms of numerals and words.
3. Writing numbers 11–19 in the forms of both numerals and words.
4. Writing ordinal numbers, illustrating them within sets of objects, and writing them in words.

5. Writing numbers 20–99, both in numerals and words.
6. Writing numbers in hundreds, both in numerals and words.
7. Writing three-digit numbers and finding out how many hundreds, how many tens, and how many unities they contain; then writing them in expanded form so that 357 is written as $300+50+7$.
8. Repeating exercises 6 and 7 above with four-digit numbers.
9. Giving adults three to four different digits and asking them to make, with those same digits, the biggest and the smallest numbers possible.

Teaching the four arithmetical operations

Addition

Participants should be helped to understand that addition is counting and counting is itself a form of addition. A simple number line as given below can be used to show that $0+1=1$, $1+1=2$, $2+1=3$, and so on.

| 0 | 1 | 2 | 3 | 4 | 5 | 6 | 7 | 8 | 9 | .... |

This number line can also be used to show that both $6+5$ and $5+6$ make 11; that 11 can be broken into $5+6$ but also into $5+4+2$ and $8+3$, etc.

    The skill of writing numbers in their expanded form can now be put to good use in addition. To add 54 and 23 the two numbers may be expanded as $50+4$ and $20+3$. Then 50 can be added to 20 to make 70; 4 can be added to 3 to make 7; and 70 and 7 can be added to make 77. This should provide a bridge for the next step of teaching the concept of carrying over and regrouping. It must be emphasized that only numbers in like places can be added when regrouping and carrying over numbers in the process of addition. Three principles are important: (a) adding 0 to a number does not change the number; (b) we can add numbers in any order and get the same sum, and we can break a number into different parts; and (c) only numbers in like places can be added when making additions by carrying over.

    In learning addition, the following thirty-six arithmetical facts must become sight facts and, therefore, automatic with participants. These are:

$9+9=18$			
$9+8=17$	$8+8=16$		
$9+7=16$	$8+7=15$	$7+7=14$	
$9+6=15$	$8+6=14$	$7+6=13$	$6+6=12$
$9+5=14$	$8+5=13$	$7+5=12$	$6+5=11$
$9+4=13$	$8+4=12$	$7+4=11$	$6+4=10$
$9+3=12$	$8+3=11$	$7+3=10$	$6+3=9$
$9+2=11$	$8+2=10$	$7+2=9$	$6+2=8$
$5+5=10$			
$5+4=9$	$4+4=8$		
$5+3=8$	$4+3=7$	$3+3=6$	
$5+2=7$	$4+2=6$	$3+2=5$	$2+2=4$

These thirty-six additions should first be worked out in the class by the participants themselves, and then practised in class by showing the two flashcards of the numbers to be added and asking the participants what their sum will be.

The workbook must provide exercises for participants to practise their learning. Additions should not remain purely number operations. These operations should be applied to concrete situations around the home, the field and the market. A sequence to be followed for exercises in the workbook is suggested as follows: (a) additions where the sum does not exceed 10; (b) additions with one digit numbers, the sum not to exceed 18; (c) two two-digit addends, both as completed tens, such as 20, 50, etc.; (d) two addends of completed hundreds (i.e. 100, 200, 300, etc.) and completed thousands; (e) two two-digit addends not requiring regrouping or carrying; (f) two two-digit addends requiring carrying; (g) three or more two-digit (and one-digit) numbers requiring carrying; (h) two, three or more digit numbers requiring regrouping; and (i) three or more numbers with one, two or more digits requiring regrouping.

The adults should be taught, as far as possible, to verify their results. If the addends are small, verification can be done by counting. For example, $15+7=22$ can be checked by counting. Bigger sums may be checked by breaking them into different patterns in the process of adding them up and then comparing results.

Subtraction
Subtraction should be taught as the reverse of addition. The number line can, again, be used with great advantage. The instructor should spend some time teaching the principle that if 0 is subtracted from a number, the number remains the same—thus $9-0=9$. The principle that if a number is deducted from itself the remainder is 0 should also be taught—

thus $33 - 33 = 0$. It should also be reinforced that only numbers in like places can be deducted from each other.

The concept of carrying and regrouping taught as part of addition must now be reviewed to teach the opposite process of regrouping and borrowing in the process of subtracting.

The instructor should also give the participants some practice in one very useful device for making subtraction problems simpler—by adding or subtracting a suitable number from both numbers in a problem of subtraction. For example, while subtracting 98 from 211 one could add 2 to both these numbers to make them 100 and 213 and make the problem of subtraction much simpler. Similarly in subtracting 211 from 354 one could take out 11 from both these numbers first and reduce the problem to a simpler version (i.e. $343 - 200$) to get an answer.

For the workbook, the following sequence is recommended for exercises —remembering that the workbook must give not only arithmetical practice but also relate problems to the various spheres of the participants, lives: (a) subtraction of one-digit numbers; (b) subtraction where the larger of two numbers is not more than 18; (c) subtraction in which the larger number is in two digits, and the lower number may be in one or two digits, but where no borrowing is necessary; (d) as in (c) above but where borrowing is necessary; (e) subtraction involving hundreds—first with no borrowing necessary and then with borrowing necessary both of unities and tens; and (f) subtraction of both types with higher numbers.

As we mentioned in the case of addition, the participants should themselves try to verify their answers. This can be done in two ways. If the numbers involved are small, subtraction may be verified simply by counting back. In bigger subtraction, the result may be added to the smaller of the two numbers of subtraction to see if it adds up to the larger number.

Multiplication

Multiplication should first be introduced by the instructor as the process of addition, where one number is added to another a certain number of times. Thus, if I buy four kilograms of sugar, when a kilogram costs 5 rupees, we can find the total in this way:

5 rupees for the first kilogram
5 rupees for the second kilogram
5 rupees for the third kilogram
5 rupees for the fourth kilogram

———————————————————————

20 rupees for four kilograms

But, we often shorten this operation by writing this arithmetical sentence: $5 \times 4 = 20$, that is to say, the number 5 repeated 4 times, in other words, 4 times 5 is 20. If we buy 7 kilograms of sugar at the same price, then $5 \times 7 = 35$.

However, we cannot handle all multiplications as additions. That process would be cumbersome. The participants in literacy classes must, therefore, be taught the simple rules of multiplication. The participants should be introduced to the sign of multiplication— $\times$. The words 'factor' and 'product' must also be introduced. Numbers entering into any multiplication are called factors and what is obtained is a product. Thus, in $5 \times 7 = 35$, 5 and 7 are both factors and 35 is the product.

The instructor must teach the following rules of multiplication, using concrete examples to bring out generalizations: (a) a number multiplied by 1 remains the same. (If we buy 1 kilogramme of sugar at the rate of 5 rupees per kilogramme, we pay $1 \times 5 = 5$ rupees.); (b) a number multiplied by 0 gives the product zero. (If we bought no sugar at the rate of 5 rupees per kilogramme, we paid $0 \times 5 = 0$ rupees, i.e. we paid nothing.); (c) whatever the order of factors in a multiplication, the product remains the same, thus $5 \times 4 = 20$, also $4 \times 5 = 20$. (This, again, the instructor can demonstrate by taking concrete examples.); and (d) multiplication equations, such as $5 \times 15 = 75$, can be written in expanded forms as $5 \times (10 + 5) = 75$. This is called 'factorization' and may be put to many concrete uses.

By using a set of asterisks, as in Figure 2, the instructor could demonstrate the process of factorization and show various relationships.

FIGURE 2. *The process of factorization*

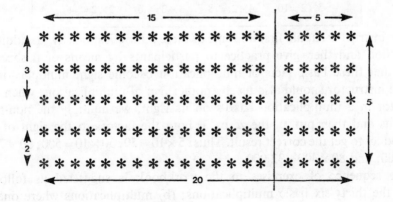

$5 \times 20 = 100$ $(2+3) \times 20 = 100$
$5 \times (20-5) = 75$ $(2+3) \times (10+5) = 75$

The instructor should now explain how the algorithm of multiplication
is obtained from rule (d) above. Take two factors, 27×35. In the expanded
form, we can write the product as follows: $(20+7) \times (30+5)$

$$= 20 \times 30 + 20 \times 5 + 7 \times 30 + 7 \times 5$$
$$= \quad 600 + \quad 100 \quad + \quad 210 \quad + \quad 35 \quad = 945.$$

By abbreviating this operation as follows we get the multiplication
algorithm.

$$\begin{array}{r} 35 \\ 27 \\ \hline 245 \\ 70 \\ \hline 945 \end{array}$$

The first operation here $35 \times 7 = 245$ gives the sum of the last
two numbers of the multiplication in the expanded form. The
second operation 2×35 (which is really $20 \times 35 = 700$) gives
us the first two numbers of the expanded form. The result
in both cases is 945.

Under the section on 'Addition' we introduced thirty-six arithmetical facts
which must become automatic with participants in order to master
addition. Similarly, there are thirty-six arithmetical facts that must become
automatic with the participants for the mastery of multiplications:

$9 \times 9 = 81$			
$9 \times 8 = 72$	$8 \times 8 = 64$		
$9 \times 7 = 63$	$8 \times 7 = 56$	$7 \times 7 = 49$	
$9 \times 6 = 54$	$8 \times 6 = 48$	$7 \times 6 = 42$	$6 \times 6 = 36$
$9 \times 5 = 45$	$8 \times 5 = 40$	$7 \times 5 = 35$	$6 \times 5 = 30$
$9 \times 4 = 36$	$8 \times 4 = 32$	$7 \times 4 = 28$	$6 \times 4 = 24$
$9 \times 3 = 27$	$8 \times 3 = 24$	$7 \times 3 = 21$	$6 \times 3 = 18$
$9 \times 2 = 18$	$8 \times 2 = 16$	$7 \times 2 = 14$	$6 \times 2 = 12$
$5 \times 5 = 25$			
$5 \times 4 = 20$	$4 \times 4 = 16$		
$5 \times 3 = 15$	$4 \times 3 = 12$	$3 \times 3 = 9$	
$5 \times 2 = 10$	$4 \times 2 = 8$	$3 \times 2 = 6$	$2 \times 2 = 4$

The instructor should first do some of these multiplications by the addition
method and then give practice to participants by means of flashcards,
so that these basic facts of multiplication become sight multiplications.
The instructor should also teach another fact of multiplication: when any
factor in a multiplication has 0s on its right, we multiply the non-zero
digits and then put all the zeros in both the factors to the right of the
product to get the correct result. Thus: $5 \times 10 = 50$; $50 \times 10 = 500$; $50 \times 70 =$
$3\,500$; and $80 \times 400 = 32\,000$.
The sequence of exercises in the workbook is suggested as follows:
(a) the thirty-six basic multiplications; (b) multiplications where one of

the factors is a one-digit number and the other factor is a ten or a hundred, or where both factors are in tens, hundreds, etc.; (c) multiplications where one factor is a one-digit number and the other factor is any number with two digits. (This kind of exercise is meant to give practice in multiplication by taking the two-digit number in an expanded form. Later, three- or four-digit numbers can be multiplied by a one-digit number); (d) both factors are two-digit numbers. (At first, multiplication by taking numbers in their expanded form; later, using the multiplication method); and (e) taking large numbers and utilizing the multiplication method.

Participants should be encouraged to verify their multiplications. With small numbers they can check by counting. Later, they should check using rule (d) (in the first part of this section), i.e. by breaking up one or both numbers in a different way than given in the exercise. When participants have learnt division they can check their multiplications by dividing the product by one of the factors to see if this operation yields the other factor.

Division

The instructor should first of all explain that just as subtraction is, in a way, the inverse of addition, so also is division the inverse of multiplication. Thus, to divide 72 by 9, we use our knowledge of basic multiplication facts to find the number which, when multiplied with 8, will gives us 72. There are three symbols which tell us that the problem is one of division. For example, the division of 72 by 9, can be written in one of these three ways:

$$72 \div 9, \quad \frac{72}{9} \quad \text{and} \quad 9 \overline{\smash{\big)}\,72.}$$

The solution in all these three cases will be 8. The number 72 in this division is called the 'dividend', 9 is called the 'divisor' and the result of division, in this case 8, is called the 'quotient'.

If we substituted 73 for 72 to have $73 \div 9$, then we would also have a 'remainder', 1. The instructor should also make the meaning of division clear to his class by showing that: (a) it is dividing a number of things (dividend) *equally* among a certain number of people (divisor); and (b) it is a form of repeated subtraction of a number (divisor) from another bigger number (dividend)—the number of subtractions stops when the divisor cannot be further deducted from the dividend, thus giving the quotient.

The instructor should teach the following rules of division, using concrete examples to bring out generalizations: (a) if we divide a dividend by 1, what remains is the dividend itself; (b) if we divide the dividend by the dividend itself, what remains is 1; (c) in ordinary everyday life dividing a dividend by zero does not make much sense. Dividing zero by a number, as in $0 \div 5$, gives zero; and (d) as the concept of factorization in multiplication provided the multiplication algorithm, factorization again provides the algorithm for the division. For example,

$$\frac{144}{12} = \frac{120+24}{12} = \frac{120}{12} + \frac{24}{12} = 10+2 = 12.$$

It can then be used to explain why we do what we do when using the division algorithm, as in the following:

$$
\begin{array}{r}
12 \\
12 \overline{)144} \\
12 \\
\hline
24 \\
24 \\
\hline
\text{x}
\end{array}
$$

A useful device in simplifying division is to eliminate any factor that is common between the dividend and the divisor:

$$\text{thus } \frac{24}{9} = \frac{8 \times 3}{3 \times 3}$$

Eliminating the common factor '3' from both the dividend and the divisor reduces $\frac{24}{9}$ to $\frac{8}{3}$.

The instructor's guide should include more detailed discussion of the conceptual basis of the division (as well as of the multiplication) algorithm. Within the scope of this monograph we are able to include only the barest minimum of details that must be covered in an instructor's guide. It is important, however, to say something here about 'estimating' which occupies a very important place in understanding division.

Let us take the problem $64\,766 \div 13$. Writing the dividend in the expanded form we can write it as follows:

$$\frac{60\,000+4'000+700+60+6}{13} = \frac{60\,000}{13} + \frac{4\,000}{13} + \frac{700}{13} + \frac{60}{13} + \frac{6}{13}.$$

We have now to estimate the quotient in each of these divisions. Thus, we know that $13 \times 5 = 65$, so 5 cannot be the quotient of 60,000. It can only be 4. So, $13 \times 4\,000 = 52\,000$, and $60\,000 = 52\,000 + 8\,000$.

The dividend now reads: $\dfrac{52\ 000}{13}+\dfrac{8\ 000}{13}+\dfrac{4\ 000}{13}+\dfrac{700}{13}+\dfrac{60}{13}+\dfrac{6}{13}$

$$=4\ 000+\dfrac{12\ 000}{13}+\dfrac{700}{13}+\dfrac{60}{13}+\dfrac{6}{13}.$$

We now have to tackle $\dfrac{12\ 000}{13}$.

We will again make an estimate. The best estimate is $13\times9=117$, so that $13\times900=11\ 700$, and $12\ 000=11\ 700+300$. So we write the division as:

$$4\ 000+\dfrac{11\ 700}{13}+\dfrac{300}{13}+\dfrac{700}{13}+\dfrac{60}{13}+\dfrac{6}{13}=4\ 000+900+\dfrac{1\ 000}{13}+\dfrac{66}{13}.$$

Now we have to tackle $\dfrac{1\ 000}{13}$.

Again we make an estimate. The best estimate is $13\times7=91$. So we write:

$$\dfrac{1\ 000}{13}=\dfrac{910+90}{13}=70+\dfrac{90}{13}.$$

We re-write the quotient thus:

$$4\ 000+900+70+\dfrac{90}{13}+\dfrac{66}{13},\ \text{or}\ 4\ 970+\dfrac{156}{13}.$$

Now $\dfrac{156}{13}=\dfrac{130}{13}+\dfrac{26}{13}=10+2=12.$

So the quotient comes to $4\ 970+12=4\ 982$. So that $64\ 766\div13=4\ 982$. To check our answer we know that dividend=divisor×quotient. Therefore, we do the multiplication $13\times4\ 982$. We get the product as $64\ 766$, which shows that our division is correct.

In the workbook, the sequence of exercises on division will be as follows: (a) division where the divisor is any number from 2 to 9, and the dividend is in tens—first without 0, then with 0. (There should be no remainder); (b) as in (a), but now there is a remainder; (c) dividend in hundreds, the quotient being any number from 2 to 9. (The exercise requires estimating); (d) divisor is a two-digit number, where the dividend will give a one-digit quotient; (e) practice in estimating; (f) divisor is a two-digit number, dividend a multiple of 10, quotient in two digits; (g) the same as above, but dividend is *not* a multiple of 10. (The dividend may first be in two digits, then in three digits and then in four digits); (h) divisor in three digits, being a multiple of 10 or 100; dividend, first a multiple of 10, then 100, no remainder; (i) as (h), but the divisor is not a multiple of 10 or

100. (It may by any three-digit number, no remainder); and (j) the same as (i), but with remainder.

In all the four arithmetical operations—addition, subtraction, multiplication and division—the instructor must carry out, with the help of participants, an adequate number of exercises in the sequences mentioned above under each operation. The rules given for each operation should first be learnt in concrete situations and then expressed in arithmetical symbols. Participants should be advised to check their results according to the suggestions given in each section. Each type of number exercise should be followed in the workbook by exercises resembling problems in the day-to-day life of the participants.

Teaching fractions

The instructor of a literacy group should make clear to the participants the following facts about fractions: (a) what they are; (b) how we tell which of any two fractions is the bigger; (c) how the same fraction can be written in different ways; and (d) how we can add, subtract, multiply and divide fractions.

We have indicated before that the teaching of arithmetic is an area where literacy instructors themselves need considerable help. Therefore, the instructor's guide must include a detailed set of instructions on how to teach fractions and the arithmetical processes involving fractions.

The instructors themselves should be helped to understand the concept of real fractions—an infinite series of numbers that are more than 0, but less than 1, such as $\frac{1}{2}$, $\frac{1}{3}$, $\frac{1}{4}$, $\frac{9}{11}$, $\frac{79}{101}$, etc. He should also be introduced to the concept of 'numerator' (the number above the bar in a fraction) and 'denominator' (the number below the bar).

The instructor's guide should also include detailed suggestions on the use of bar graphs and pie charts to explain the meanings of common fractions, such as $\frac{1}{2}$, $\frac{1}{3}$, $\frac{1}{4}$, $\frac{1}{8}$ and $\frac{1}{6}$.

Just as a number can be written in many kinds of numerals or combination of numerals, so can the fraction be written differently. Let us take the fraction $\frac{1}{2}$ which, because it is a number, permits the application of all rules relating to the four arithmetical operations. Thus $\frac{1}{2} \times 1 = \frac{1}{2}$. Again, as 1 can be written as $\frac{2}{2}$ or $\frac{3}{3}$ or $\frac{4}{4}$, etc., similarly, $\frac{1}{2}$ can be written as $\frac{1}{2} \times \frac{2}{2}$ or $\frac{1}{2} \times \frac{3}{3}$ or $\frac{1}{2} \times \frac{4}{4}$, etc. That is to say, $\frac{1}{2} = \frac{2}{4} = \frac{3}{6} = \frac{4}{8}$, etc. Fractions like $\frac{1}{2}$, $\frac{2}{4}$, $\frac{3}{6}$ and $\frac{4}{8}$, which really are one and the same number, are called equivalent fractions. The instructor should bring home to his literacy group the idea of equivalent fractions through bar diagrams.

In teaching the addition and subtraction of fractions, the rule that fractions can be added or subtracted only if they have common denominators must be explained. Taking two fractions, the denominators can easily be made the same in the two fractions by multiplying *both* the numerator and the denominator of each fraction by the denominator of the other fraction. The two new fractions thus obtained will be equivalent fractions of the two original fractions and yet can be easily added by simply adding the numerators of the two new fractions to get the numerator and using the common denominator as the denominator to obtain the sum of two fractions. The same strategy is applied in subtracting one fraction from another. In this case, the smaller numerator would be subtracted from the other to obtain the solution. The strategy for obtaining common denominators when more than two fractions are involved in addition or subtraction should also be taught to literacy classes.

In teaching multiplication of fractions, use may again be made of graphics. For example, $\frac{2}{3} \times \frac{1}{4} = \frac{1}{6}$ can be demonstrated by a simple diagram such as the following:

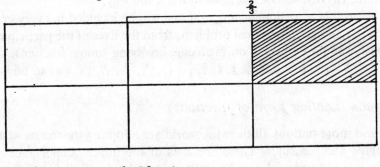

$\frac{2}{3} \times \frac{1}{4}$ = $\frac{1}{4}$ of $\frac{2}{3}$ and $\frac{1}{6}$ of 1

The multiplication algorithm for fractions can be introduced then as:

$$\frac{\text{numerator} \times \text{numerator}}{\text{denominator} \times \text{denominator}}.$$

In teaching division involving fractions, again, graphics should be used. For example, we can illustrate $\frac{3}{4} \div \frac{1}{2}$ as follows:

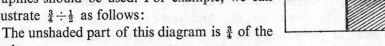

The unshaded part of this diagram is $\frac{3}{4}$ of the total.

The basic question in this operation is: how many times can we take $\frac{1}{2}$ out of $\frac{3}{4}$ or how many $\frac{1}{2}$'s are there in $\frac{3}{4}$. Further inspection of the diagram tells us that we can take a $\frac{1}{2}$ (of the total) out of $\frac{3}{4}$, $1\frac{1}{2}$ times, which can be numerically presented as $\frac{1}{2}+\frac{1}{2}+\frac{1}{2}=\frac{3}{2}$.

This gives us the algorithm for dividing fractions, namely, invert the divisor and multiply with the resulting fraction. Thus

$$\tfrac{3}{4} \div \tfrac{1}{2} = \tfrac{3}{4} \times \tfrac{2}{1} = \tfrac{6}{4} = \tfrac{3 \times 2}{2 \times 2} = \tfrac{3}{2}.$$

The sequence of exercises may be as follows: (a) understanding what a real fraction is with the help of drawings; (b) understanding what we mean by the numerator and the denominator; (c) understanding which fraction is greater than another if the denominators of both are the same; (d) what are equivalent fractions?—understanding from graphs and by multiplication by appropriate numbers; (e) addition of fractions—taking first a whole number and a fraction, then both addends as fractions; understanding the algorithm of adding a fraction first through graphs and later by numbers; (f) subtracting one fraction from another as in (e) above; (g) understanding the multiplication of fractions as in (e) above— that is to say, first taking a whole number and a fraction, then both fractions; also understanding first from graphs and then arriving at the algorithm; (h) division of fractions in the same way.

As before, these arithmetical operations will be included in every group of exercises as well as practical problems from the lives of the participants. Emphasis should be placed on problems involving simple fractions, such as, $\frac{1}{2}, \frac{1}{3}, \frac{2}{3}, \frac{1}{4}, \frac{3}{4}, \frac{1}{5}, \frac{2}{5}, \frac{1}{6}, \frac{3}{6}, \frac{4}{6}, \frac{5}{6}, \frac{1}{8}, \frac{3}{8}, \frac{5}{8}, \frac{1}{12}, \frac{2}{12}, \frac{3}{12}, \frac{4}{12}, \frac{5}{12}, \frac{6}{12}$, and so on.

Decimals: another form of fractions

More and more nations all over the world are adopting the metric system of weights and measures. Therefore, it is of the utmost importance that participants in literacy classes be assisted in understanding and mastering the decimal system.

The instructor when teaching decimal fractions should start with the system of counting, thus: a thousand=ten times a hundred; a hundred= ten times ten; ten=ten times unity. In counting we stopped here because we were then concerned with whole numbers, but when dealing with fractions, we go beyond or below unities, thus: unity=ten times $\frac{1}{10}$; $\frac{1}{10}=$ ten times $\frac{1}{100}$; $\frac{1}{100}=$ten times $\frac{1}{1000}$. And, just as a numeral represents tens or hundreds or thousands depending on its place in a number as it is written, so also, when we go below unities, it is the place of a numeral which tells us whether it represents $\frac{1}{10}$ or $\frac{1}{100}$ or $\frac{1}{1000}$. In order to know that unities end here and fractions begin, we place a full stop between the

unities and fractions. This full stop is called the decimal point. With this full stop we write $\frac{1}{10}$ as ·1; $\frac{1}{100}$ as ·01; and $\frac{1}{1000}$ as ·001. Thus, if we take a number such as 4321·237, in expanded form it will be written as:
$$4000+300+20+1+\tfrac{2}{10}+\tfrac{3}{100}+\tfrac{7}{1000}.$$
In this example ·237 is called a 'decimal fraction'. As an ordinary fraction it would be written as $\frac{237}{1000}$—as many zeros in the denominator as there are digits to the right of the decimal point. Thus, ·08 $=\frac{8}{100}$ and ·008 $=\frac{8}{1000}$. Graphically, we may illustrate the decimal system as follows:

thousands	hundreds	tens	unities	tenths	hundredths	thousandths

The instructor's guide should tell the instructor to work out with the class decimal equivalents of common ordinary fractions, for instance $\frac{1}{2}=$·5, $\frac{1}{4}=$·25, $\frac{3}{4}=$·75, etc.

Addition and subtraction
There are no differences in addition and subtraction between whole numbers and decimals. However, participants must take care to see that the decimal points of the numbers involved are put one below the other as follows:

$$\begin{array}{r} 5{\cdot}25 \\ +10{\cdot}05 \\ \hline 15{\cdot}30 \end{array} \qquad\qquad \begin{array}{r} 10{\cdot}05 \\ -\ 5{\cdot}25 \\ \hline 4{\cdot}80 \end{array}$$

In subraction, some difficulty may arise if the lower number has more decimal digits than the upper number, as in the following:

$$\begin{array}{r} 7{\cdot}5 \\ -\ 3{\cdot}05 \end{array}$$

In such cases, we put as many zeros after the decimal figure in the upper number as are required to even the figures up. This is possible because ·5, ·50, ·500 or ·5000, etc., is actually the same number. This becomes obvious if we change these decimal fractions into ordinary fractions. We can see that ·5$=\frac{5}{10}$, ·50$=\frac{50}{100}$, ·500$=\frac{500}{1000}$, etc., all of which can be reduced to $\frac{1}{2}$. That being so, we can write the above subtraction as:

$$\begin{array}{r} 7{\cdot}50 \\ -\ 3{\cdot}05 \\ \hline 4{\cdot}45 \end{array}$$

Multiplication
In multiplying numbers with decimals, we multiply them as in ordinary multiplications and then put the decimal point in the product at a point where the number of decimal digits will be the sum of the number of decimal digits in *both* fractions. Take, for example, 5·5 × 2·75. Forgetting

decimals, we multiply 55×275 to get 15125. We see that there is one decimal digit in 5·5 and two in 2·75, making three decimal digits in all. So we put the decimal point three digits from the right in the number 15125, thereby getting 15·125.

Division

In division involving decimal numbers, care must be taken to see that the decimal point in the quotient is in the same place as the decimal point in the dividend. However, before doing the actual division, see that there is no decimal left in the divisor. This is easily done by the device of equivalent fractions. Thus:

$$\frac{15 \cdot 125}{2 \cdot 75} = \frac{15 \cdot 125}{2 \cdot 75} \times \frac{100}{100} = \frac{1512 \cdot 5}{275}.$$

The division can now proceed as follows:

$$
\begin{array}{r}
5 \cdot 5 \\
275 \overline{\smash{)}\ 1512 \cdot 5} \\
1375 \\
\hline
1375 \\
1375 \\
\hline
-
\end{array}
$$

Decimal exercises

In the workbook the following types of exercises should be given:

1. Changing some common fractions into decimal fractions and vice versa.
2. Adding two decimal numbers: (a) where both numbers have the same number of decimal places; (b) where one number has one more decimal place than the other; (c) where one of the numbers has no decimal fraction in it; (d) where one or both numbers are only decimal fractions; (e) as in (d) above, but one or both numbers have one or more zeros after the decimal point.
3. Subtraction, as in (a) to (e) above.
4. Multiplication: (a) where one of the numbers is a whole number; (b) where both numbers have decimal fractions; (c) where both numbers are only decimal fractions.
5. Division: (a) where the divisor is a whole number; (b) where both the dividend and divisor contain decimal fractions; (c) where the quotient is to be given approximately.

Teaching proportions

Proportions are best introduced as two equivalent fractions. For example, $\frac{3}{4}=\frac{9}{12}$. This can also be written as $\frac{3}{4}:\frac{9}{12}$; that is $\frac{3}{4}$ is proportional to $\frac{9}{12}$. The workbook should include exercises that demonstrate the use of proportions in everyday life.

Percentages should be also explained as fractions: $\frac{8}{100}$ means 8 parts out of 100, or 8 per cent. The percentage sign (%) should be introduced. There are thus three types of fractions: ordinary fractions ($\frac{3}{4}$); decimal fractions (·75); and percentages (75%). The instructor's guide should include material on processes of converting decimals into percentages, percentages into decimals, ordinary fractions into percentages and percentages into ordinary fractions. There should also be exercises on computing profit and loss on sales and purchases, and other problems likely to be met by the participants in every day life.

The workbook may include the following types of exercises:

1. Different forms of figures—a bar, a circle, a square—with shaded and unshaded parts to test the concept of percentages.
2. Conversion of ordinary fractions, decimal fractions and percentages into one another, as in the following:

Fractions	$\frac{1}{5}$			$\frac{1}{4}$		
Decimals		·75				·6
Percentages			30%		75%	

3. Questions concerning the percentage of loss or profit, going from simple questions to somewhat more complicated. For example: A peasant spent on his crop the following sums:

   For seed   ...   Irrigation   ...
   For help in ploughing   ...   Depreciation   ...
   Fertilizers   ...

   His yield was ... kilogrammes, which he sold for ... rupees per kilogramme. What was the percentage for his profit or loss?
4. Questions concerning loans may also be included. For example: A man got a loan for ... rupees for a period of ... at a rate of interest of ...%. What interest will he have to pay? Or, what is the sum he will have to give back after the period of loan is over?

Working with measurements

In everyday life we have to measure many things—lengths, distances, weights, etc. Some we measure directly, such as length and area, while others, like time and temperature, we measure indirectly. Before the instructor deals with these measurements, he should discuss with the participants the following points:

1. We measure things by taking a specific measure as a unit.
2. Some units of measurements, such as length, are comparable to the things measured. Others, such as temperature, are indirect and unlike the things measured.
3. Social and economic life requires that units of measurement should be fixed and not vary from man to man or place to place. Units of measurements which all men in a society accept are called 'standard units' or 'standards of measurement'. Now, gradually, various units of measurement in length and weight are becoming universal—for example, the metric system.
4. Smaller units of measurement give more precise measurements than larger units; both kinds of units are necessary. For example, if we measure the length of a room, we may not be able to measure it exactly in whole metres—the last metre may fall short of the length of the room or may be more than it. Hence, along with metres, we can also give the length in centimetres. In fact, millimetres will give the length even more precisely. But, except perhaps for some scientific measurements, no measurement can be 'absolutely' correct. Men have to accept the nearest approximation on which they can agree.

The instructor should give the participants a good deal of practice on common measurements. These are: (a) length or distance; (b) area; (c) volume; (d) capacity; (e) money; (f) weight; and (g) time. The following basic information must be included in the instructor's guide.

Length or distance

We measure length by placing the unit of measurement alongside the thing to be measured. The unit of length accepted almost all over the world is the metre. For example, we measure cloth by metres. For long distances, such as, distance between two cities, we measure in kilometres; for short lengths we measure in centimetres and even in millimetres. For example, the length of a page of a book may be measured in centimetres and millimetres. The relation between the standards of measurement mentioned above is as follows: 1,000 metres = 1 kilometre; 100 centimetres = 1 metre; 10 millimetres = 1 centimetre. Thus, we see that a metre = ·001 kilometres; 1 millimetre = ·1 centimetres = ·001 metres.

Area
This is the measurement of surfaces. The units are squares of various sizes. For smaller surfaces, such as the page of a book, square centimetres are used; for larger areas, such as rooms and carpets, square metres are used; for measuring land we usually use hectares=10,000 square metres. For a surface which has four sides, such that two opposite sides are equal and adjacent sides are at right-angles, we find the area by multiplying the length by breadth or width. We say that the formula for such areas $=l \times w$ (*l* for length, *w* for width). The instructor should make these ideas concrete by actual measurements of some conveniently measurable surface.

Volume
A box or a room is also measured in metres and centimetres, and is expressed in cubics. Volume of a room will be its area×its height. The formula for volume is $l \times w \times h$, where *l* is length, *w* is width or breadth and *h* is height. The volume of liquids is measured in cubic centimetres and litres. One litre=1,000 cubic centimetres; 1 cubic centimetre is written as 1 cc.

Money
Each country has its own standards of money, but the United States dollar is internationally accepted as a unit of money for transactions. A dollar=100 cents. A cent is ·01 dollar. Many countries are now using the metric system for their money. Thus, in India a rupee=100 paise, or 1 paisa = ·01 rupees.

Weight
Weight is now measured in grammes and kilogrammes—grammes for smaller weights, and kilogrammes for bigger weights. 1000 grammes= 1 kilogramme.

Time
Time is directly measured in days and phases of the moon. But, nowadays, time is measured indirectly. Time within a day is measured by the movement of the hands of a clock or a watch. Yearly time is measured by the dates on a calendar. The units of measurement of time are: one year= twelve months; one month=thirty days for April, June, September and November, thirty-one days for January, March, May, July, August, October and December, and twenty-nine days for February when the

number of a year is divisible by four (e.g. 1972, 1976, etc.), otherwise twenty-eight days; one day=twenty-four hours; one hour=sixty minutes; and one minute=sixty seconds.

The arithmetic workbook should give two types of exercises in measurement. First, it should teach the relation between measures belonging to one category. For example, 5 cm. = ... metres; 7 metres = ... kilometres, and vice versa. Such questions should be given for all the seven types of measurement given here. Second, it should give practical problems of concern to group members on all the seven types of measurement.

It remains to be said that both the instructor's guide as well as the arithmetic workbook should include revisions after every five to seven lessons. The revisions may concentrate on the lessons between the previous revision lesson and the current revision lesson, and may even include exercises of the types tackled prior to the last revision lesson.

Summary

The sole purpose of arithmetic is counting. Counting is done with the help of numbers, which are names for sequential facts, and quantities of such facts. Numbers are best taught by the number line. We are able to write an infinite variety of numbers by grouping the numerals 0, 1, 2, 3, 4, 5, 6, 7, 8 and 9 in hierarchies of ten so that the same numeral can have different place values. Man's developing skills in counting have materialized in the form of four basic arithmetical operations: addition, subtraction, multiplication and division. All arithmetical operations are based on seventy-two arithmetical facts, which should become automatic with adult learners if mastery of these operations is to be assured. There are three types of fractions: ordinary fractions, decimals, and percentages; and for mastery of numeracy one must be able to work with these fractions as well as with proportions and units of measurement of length, area, volume, weight, time and speed. Arithmetic is a highly structured language system and, therefore, exercises in the workbook need to be carefully sequenced. Also, since the teaching of arithmetic requires special skills, the instructor's guide should include detailed instructions to assist the instructor in the task of teaching arithmetic to the participants in adult literacy classes.

CHAPTER EIGHT

Reading to learn:
literacy in the second spiral

If work in the first spiral has been done well, it will prepare the participants for transition from the phase of learning to read to the phase of reading to learn. By the time the learner is ready for the second spiral, he will have developed the following literacy skills:

1. He will have acquired a vocabulary of 150-200 sight words, selected on the basis of the frequency of their occurrence in conversations on the subject of concern to participants.
2. In fact, by recognition of inflections of sight words and by understanding the role played by prefixes and suffixes in modifying the meaning of words, he will have a reading vocabulary of nearly 1,000 words.
3. He will have acquired the skill to write not only the words which he can read, but also other common words, except those words with unusual spellings.
4. He will have acquired some skill in understanding a piece of writing by means of silent reading.
5. He will also have acquired fluency in reading with understanding.
6. If the language in which he has learned to read and write has a simple dictionary, he will have acquired the skill to consult a dictionary.
7. He would be able to follow simple instructions put down in a written form.
8. He will have developed the ability to decode new words not seen before, and be able to use clues, contexts and illustrations to guess or determine their meanings.
9. He will have acquired the skill to make summaries or outlines of what he reads. That is to say, he will be able to locate the main ideas in what he reads.

10. He will have understood arithmetical relations and will have acquired the skill to use these arithmetical relations in solving his everyday computational problems.
11. He will have acquired the ability to interpret simple charts, drawings and diagrams.

Learning objectives for the second spiral

In the second spiral, the main task will be to place on a sound footing the learner's ability to read in order to learn new ideas and information. This means that the learner should strengthen some of the skills learned in the first spiral and develop some new learning skills. We may list these new skills as follows:

1. He should be able to follow more complicated instructions in writing, which means that he should be able to work out a sequence of things to be done as required in a written set of instructions.
2. He should be able to use the available dictionaries of his language and go deeper into the roots of words.
3. He should be able to get behind a piece of writing to understand the mood or purpose of the author.
4. He should be able to adjust his speed of reading (and sometimes of skipping) to the purpose he has in view. For example, if he wants to follow a recipe, he should read the instructions slowly to be able to do all the things that need to be done. If he is in search of a simple fact given in a piece of writing, he may go fast and even skip through the passage to get the needed information quickly.
5. He will be able to separate the facts which go to support a certain idea from those which go against an idea or principle in a written argument.
6. He should be able to use the contents page of a book (or the index, if the book has one) to know if the information he is seeking would be found in the book.
7. He should be able to compare and contrast the ideas of different writers who have written on the same subject.
8. He should be able to use simple graphs and more complicated charts.
9. He should be able to use his arithmetical skills in different situations in his life, such as keeping his accounts, working out his expenditures and gains in his business or occupation.

10. He should be able to use his writing skills for various purposes, such as writing letters and filling in forms which it may be necessary for him to complete in the course of his occupational life.

11. He should be able to write fluently, neatly, and in letters and words of small size in straight lines.

12. In general, he should be able to use his literacy skills in all the various spheres of his life.

There is no doubt that, in the second spiral as well as in the first, the adult learner should be offered a regular, well-structured course of reading and writing. However, the participant must diversify his reading and writing and go beyond the mere requirements of the course. In developing countries, books to read are not always available and opportunities to write are also not too frequent. However, the participant must be encouraged to do the best possible in the circumstances.

Reading materials for the second spiral

The regular second spiral course should be a series of pamphlets that treats the same subject as was dealt with in the first spiral, but going into greater detail. Or these pamphlets may treat different aspects of the same subject, or subjects of like nature. If the pamphlets treat the same subject as the one treated in the first spiral, the pamphlets may be put together in the form of a book; otherwise they should be kept as separate pamphlets.

Each pamphlet—of fifty pages or so—should have at the end questions to be answered, or exercises to be carried out by the participants. Suitable space should be provided for answering these questions and tackling the exercises. Sometimes some extra pages may be left blank at the end of each pamphlet. If the pamphlet itself is divided into chapters, the questions or exercises to be done by the participants should follow each chapter. The guide for instructors should also be provided and should follow a corresponding pattern—that is to say, if a pamphlet is divided into chapters, the instructor's guide should also provide separate instructions for each chapter.

In order to illustrate these suggestions, we shall give some examples of second spiral materials. In a set of reading materials for industrial workers in Liberia, the first spiral was mainly concerned with safety and tidiness in the workshop. The second spiral had separate pamphlets—one each on simple metallurgy and use of hand tools, electricity, trade unions and mechanical drawing. As the instructors for this course were themselves supervisors in their factories, no instructor's guide was prepared, except for the pamphlet on mechanical drawing. However, 'workbook material' was included in all pamphlets.

In a literacy programme for farmers in Afghanistan, the first spiral dealt with one kind of agricultural produce, while the second spiral treated the cultivation of the same produce, but in greater detail, in ten separate small pamphlets. The second spiral materials for another course for farmers took up different crops in separate pamphlets. Questions to be answered or exercises to be done were given at the end of each pamphlet for both types of course. Instructor's guides prepared for the courses gave general and specific hints to instructors as well as exercises to be done in the class sessions.

The reading materials in the second spiral need not be subjected to any overt limitations of vocabulary. But the language used should be such as is normally spoken by the social group from which the participants are drawn. Usually, this kind of vocabulary lies between two to three thousand words from the top of the frequency scale. The word frequency of languages spoken in the developing countries has often not been studied. Therefore, the typical checks on the frequency of words in speech cannot be applied. The writer of materials must use common sense and remember that his principal task is to make himself understood by the audience. If, however, the use of some out-of-the-way words becomes necessary—and it will often become necessary—to do justice to the technical aspect of the subject matter, such words should be explained in the reading unit itself where such words first occur. Or a glossary may be supplied at the end of the pamphlet. If this is not done, the instructor should ask the participants to look up the word in the dictionary—if the group has one. As a last resort, the instructor will be there to explain the words. The use of proverbs current in the language of the audience will certainly enliven the reading text for the participants.

We have said above that the use of out-of-the-way words will become necessary in view of the nature of the learning tasks in the second spiral. The second spiral materials will have more technical, scientific, social, economic—perhaps even political and geographic—content in them than the first spiral materials. For example, in a programme for farmers, while the first spiral materials advised the farmers on crop rotation, the detailed reasons why this was necessary were given at length in the second spiral materials.

To take another example from a literacy course for housewives, the first spiral may deal with the types of foods an adult man or woman or a growing child should have. The second spiral will find it necessary to go deeper into the food intake of family members; it will talk of calories, proteins and carbohydrates, minerals and vitamins, etc. It will talk of the part they play in body metabolism and in maintaining the body in health and vigour. It may also talk of food shortages—almost every country of high illiteracy also happens to be plagued with food shortages—its causes, and ways to economize on food without jeopardizing the health of family members. It may also deal with the need for consumer associations to create a social force against profiteering in food, and to check adulteration and maldistribution of things which a family may need for a minimum, but adequate, standard of living. Such a scope and level of discussion will need a large vocabulary and special words.

The development of subject matter for the second spiral needs no new effort on the part of a team of instructional materials specialists. If the type of investigations mentioned in Chapter III, 'Developing subject-matter content', have been done well (which means that the total requirements of knowledge and skills of the population providing recruits for literacy groups have been kept in mind), it will yield content for materials for both spirals of the literacy course. It will then be up to the reading materials writer to see what part of the subject matter can be put in the first spiral, with its limitations of reading vocabulary, and what part should be left to form the content of the second spiral.

In the first spiral we had provided for separate, though integrated, materials for the teaching of arithmetic or computation. In the second spiral, both the instructor's guide and the pamphlets for readers should include exercises that involve the utilization of arithmetical relations learnt in the first spiral in concrete situations familiar to the participants. The participants may be required to calculate the quantity of seed they would need for the measure of land on which they wanted to sow sugar beet. A housewife in the literacy class may be required to work out the monthly expenditure involved in an economical, but adequate, diet for her family. It will help her to see the relevance of computational skills to her role in the family; it may, indeed, help her with her own image as a partner in housekeeping, along with the family's breadwinner. This brings out another distinctive feature of the second-spiral materials, namely, their global nature, where all the different aspects of a question—linguistic, technical, scientific, economic, social, etc.—are treated as aspects of the same problem in one place.

We have recommended that the first-spiral reading materials are best laid out in the form of a dialogue. In the second spiral, various approaches may be tried, depending on the nature of the subject matter. In subjects such as home management, raising of agricultural crops and co-operation, the dialogue may still be preferable since it provides more scope for bringing in wit and humour which, in addition to its own intrinsic attraction, can break the monotony of an extensive treatment of a subject for persons for whom reading has not yet become part of the life-style. The narrative form has merit where the subject matter has more of a logical element in it, or where the emphasis is on imparting plain information. To give an example, for a subject like preparation of an insecticide solution to be sprayed on a crop open to the risk of attack by insects, the narrative form has an advantage over other forms because it adheres strictly to the step by step procedure to be adopted in preparing the solution. Any extraneous or irrelevant element, which is more likely to come in a dialogue form, may only confuse the clear-cut presentation of a sequence of facts in preparing the solution. In subjects where there is no calendar laid down by nature, or where no sequence is inherent in the process (that is to say, where there is no logical sequence or dependence binding together the various elements of a subject matter), an alphabetical form of presentation may have an advantage. Thus, by taking the various topics in alphabetical order, the present writer prepared a thirty-three-page booklet, entitled 'My book of hand tools and metal work', for second-spiral reading in the classes organized by an industrial concern for a literacy project in Liberia. Entries under letters 'A' and 'B' were as follows:

Topic	Page	Topic	Page
Abrasives	5	Babbit	5
Alloy	5	Bearings	5
Angle gauges		Bolts	
See 'Measuring instruments'	14	See 'Screws and bolts'	22
Annealing	5	Brazening	6
Anvil	5	Buffing	6
Axle	5		

The alphabetical order was adopted in this case because, though an industrial worker should know all operations and tools dealt with in the booklet, there is no logical order among them; a class could pick up any subject which interested it on a particular day.

Finally, a programmed instruction booklet may be used to present the second-spiral material. However, in our own experience of utilizing software, programmed instruction has been problematic. Developing communities are not familiar with the technique and must first accept such materials as bonafide reading material before they can learn from them.

Whatever the form adopted, it adds to the readability of materials if the personal approach is maintained. And a direct, personal approach can be used even in dictionaries. We give here an example from the same booklet discussed earlier: *My book of hand tools and metal work.* The information under 'Anvil' was given as follows:

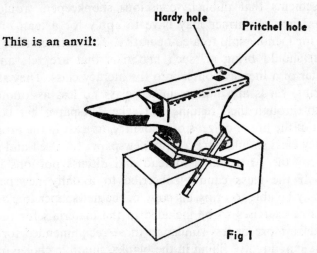

Fig 1

We hammer and cut and bend metal pieces on an anvil. Note the square hardy hole. It can hold a tool while we are working on a material. Note the round pritchel hole, it is useful for punching holes in metals and in bending small rods. An anvil weighs from 5 to 14 kilograms.
Words to remember: Hardy hole
                    Pritchel hole

The direct style with its 'we', 'you' and 'I' pronouns makes for easy reading. Whatever type of presentation of the materials is chosen, a longish text must be broken into smaller units by means of sectional headings.

The second spiral reading materials should have embedded in them as many visual aids, such as line-drawings, diagrams, pictures and charts, as are required; primarily to assist the reader in understanding the text, but also to break the monotony of the text. Graphs should be introduced wherever possible for two reasons. First, graphs help to put the subject matter given in a text in a concise form; and, second, because nowadays, graphs have become so usual in printed materials—even in newspapers—

that learning how to read graphs must be considered to have become a necessary part of a literacy course.

In our 'paperful' civilization, there is hardly any department of human life, especially in the cities, without its forms to be filled in, or its notices on the walls or in the newspapers to be read. A housewife may have to fill in some forms for ration cards, apply for milk coupons, and read prices of consumer goods through the daily newspapers as she looks at the advertisements that publicity-conscious shopkeepers would almost throw in her face. A farmer may have to apply for a loan or sign an application for membership to a co-operative. The instructor (or even the participants) should bring all such materials that are relevant to the subject-matter of a literacy course into the literacy class. They should go through forms, cards and notices in the class no less assiduously than they have to through their reading text. The newspaper has become so much a part of the life of citizens of a country, at least in the urban areas, that a literacy class should have a daily newspaper for itself and set apart some time for the participants to read and discuss portions from the newspaper. If the class cannot subscribe to a daily newspaper, the instructor may be able to bring his copy of the newspaper to class.

The types of exercises to be included in the materials for the second spiral would be more or less similar to those recommended for the first spiral. These may involve filling in the blanks, multiple-choice questions, direct questions which require answers, ticking off the correct statements out of a series, true or false choices, etc. But, in the second spiral the questions may be more complicated and may require that the answers need to be constructed using one or more sentences. For example, the question could be asked: What are the five reasons which make it necessary for you to rotate your crop? Or: Give in order the various tasks necessary for raising a wheat crop, and the times when these tasks should be done. Or the participant may be asked to complete the following chart:

Area of land to be brought under the crop.........			
Serial number	Task to be performed	Time schedule	Cost of labour and supplies
....	....	....	....
....	....	....	....
....	....	....	....

Such questions could also have been included in the first spiral, but here the answers may be more detailed and individualized.

A rhythm of work for the second spiral

The rhythm of classwork in the second spiral will be much simpler than that in the first spiral. Also, there could be a greater variety of activities. In fact the class sessions in the second spiral may resemble the sessions of a study circle more than that of a teacher-dominated class. It may be that some days could be devoted to field trips bearing on the subject of study. When that happens, the instructor should prepare the group beforehand for the type of questions the participants should bear in mind when they visit the study site in the field. After the field trip is over, he should discuss with the participants how the visit may have benefited them. The questions raised in the pre-visit discussions should again be gone over with the participants in the light of what they have learnt from the visit. Perhaps the instructor or the participants had arranged for the visit of a resource person to a group meeting, in which case, again, the pre-talk and post-talk discussions in the group will be necessary. Such events apart, the rhythm of the group work during the second spiral may be as follows:

1. If the instructor has read something of interest in the day's newspaper, he should bring the paper to the group meeting and ask one of the participants—not the same participant every time—to read the item and then ask everyone to have a brief discussion on it.

2. There should then be a discussion on the topic of the day's lesson. The instructor should see that all aspects of the problem are discussed. The instructions for conducting these discussions will have been given in the instructor's guide. The subject should be discussed in relation to the lives of the participants. Specimens of things—seeds of high-yielding varieties, tools, kitchen gadgets—should be brought to the class and seen and handled by the group members. This is also the time to use any audio-visual aids available to the group. Of course, pre-planning will be necessary in these cases. As far as possible, all new words of a technical nature should be brought up in the group discussion and learnt.

3. Following the discussion, the participants should read the lesson silently, taking such notes in their notebooks as they feel are important. If a participant comes upon a word that he cannot read or cannot understand and which blocks the understanding of the lesson, he should at once seek the help of the instructor. The instructor, if he has a dictionary with him, could ask the participant to find the word in the dictionary and see if he can then understand the sentence or the

passage. If there is no dictionary, or the participant is unable to benefit from it, the instructor should explain the word or the sentence to the participant there and then.

4. After the silent reading is over, the instructor should ask the participants questions to see if the lesson has been understood by them. Any difficulties or blocks in the understanding of the lesson by the participants should be cleared up at this time.

5. The instructor will now try to individualize the application of the things learnt in the lesson to each participant's life. If the lesson pertained, let us say, to fertilizers, each participant may be asked to work out how much fertilizer he would need for his plot of land. If it pertained to diet in a housewives' group, each woman should work out a day's meal for her family.

6. After this the group may do some writing work. This may take various forms. The teacher may dictate to the class some words on which the participants may have stumbled in part 3 above, or the words he thinks should be practised in writing. Or he may dictate a paragraph from the book, or an item from the day's newspaper which he thinks will be of interest to the participants. Or again, he may ask them to write a letter, say, to a resource person, inviting him to one of their group meetings. He may even dictate a folk song or a poem of interest to the group; or the participants may be asked to do some creative writing on any subject of their own choice. What the participants write should be examined by the instructor to see if it is correct in regard to content, form and expression. For example, in the letter inviting a resource person to give a talk, the instructor should check that the day, the time and the place for the group meeting, as well as the subject on which the group wants him to speak, are mentioned. The participants may also check what they have written among themselves. The teacher may like to read or comment on some of these texts in class, or he may take them home and give his comments when the group meets the next day.

7. Finally, the programme for the next group meeting may be discussed briefly. If some object has to be brought to the group meeting, the responsibility for bringing it may be fixed there and then. Or the instructor may ask the group members to read the next lesson once before they come to class.

As far as possible, the instructor's guide should provide help in conducting the activities suggested above. It should provide the background information required, hints on the aids and specimens which could be available to him and which he should bring into the discussion. It will provide suggestions on the type of writing he could ask the participants to do and the preparations he himself and the participants could undertake for the next lesson. The instructor can benefit from the instructor's guide only if he uses it to prepare himself for group sessions. The timely preparation for the lesson is, of course, an essential for the second spiral as it is for the first.

Wherever possible, literacy classes should establish links with the radio broadcasting service—by no means an easy task. Literacy classes should also find it useful to establish other institutional linkages for support. Some literacy classes for farmers may seek the patronage of an agricultural school; literacy classes for women may establish a link with a school or department of home economics. Literacy classes in most places may find it possible to seek help and support from an elementary school.

Some comments on the format of materials

In our discussion of instructional materials for the first spiral of literacy teaching, we have talked of seven items of instructional materials: (a) a reading text incorporating technical subject matter; (b) a workbook to go with the reading text; (c) an instructor's guide to go with the reading text and the related workbook; (d) flashcards for practising new words; (e) another workbook for teaching arithmetic; (f) a separate instructor's guide for teaching arithmetic; and (g) another set of flashcards for practising arithmetical relationships.

Those who propose (what we have called) linear integration between subject matter and literacy would propose that the reading text includes the workbook in itself; and that this workbook built into the reading text should cover exercises both on reading and arithmetic; also, that the two instructor's guides in our scheme should be put together into one. Our approach to literacy instruction separates the two processes of learning to read and write, and learning to count because of their separate logics. That is why we have chosen to separate the items of instructional materials. The reading text and the related workbook could, perhaps, be combined without doing violence to the approach, but it might make the book too cumbersome to handle. Also workbooks, if they are separate, can be examined by the instructor for different evaluative purposes and such examinations could take place without depriving the participants of their reading texts.

There is another question of format: whether the reading text and its corresponding workbook (as well as the arithmetic workbook) should be split into small booklets of twenty to thirty pages each, or whether the whole of the reading text for the first spiral should be printed in one volume. The argument of those who would split the reading text into small volumes is that a participant will have a 'glow of success' when he finishes a small text. This will help him in maintaining his reserves of morale for going through the next small volume. There is no research to back up the 'glow of success' theory. In fact, to split the reading text would segment the subject matter, damaging its unity in the minds of the participants. Also, splitting up the text into smaller portions would put an unnecessary strain on the distribution machinery.

Most first-spiral materials should be printed in bold and large type-faces. The instructor's guide, of course, need not be printed in the same large type-face. It is preferable that all items of the first spiral materials be printed on paper of uniform size. A page size of 18 cm × 23 cm has been found easy to handle by learners and able to accommodate display of both text and drawings.

In the second-spiral materials, the instructor's guide should still be separate, although everything else (reading, writing, arithmetic) could be put together in a unified reader. The page size for books now could be 15 cm × 20 cm to bring them closer to the size of books typically available in the market.

Summary

The second-spiral materials are for reading to learn. They must, therefore: (a) use a larger vocabulary of 2,000–3,000 words; (b) deal with all the different aspects—technical, scientific, economic and social—of the subject matter; and (c) use a variety of approaches in presentation from the alphabetical organization, to dialogue and to programmed instruction. The role of the instructor's guide will remain crucial in the second spiral. Some comments have been made on the format of instructional materials constituting a total system of literacy instruction.

CHAPTER NINE

Evaluation and beyond

Theoretically, a set of reading materials should be evaluated before its regular use, during its use in the programme, and after it has been used in literacy groups for its over-all impact. However, we would like to voice a reservation relating to the pre-testing of materials before their use in the programme. In the first place, there is the problem of getting a sample of population on which the material is to be tried out. If the area has had no literacy class before, or had a literacy class which was not built around a single subject-matter theme, it is not possible to decide what comparable stage of school education and what age range of population should be considered as a suitable sample. The selection and training of teachers for teaching the pre-test batch and the size of population on which the pre-test is to be made will offer further difficulties. If the population sample is small, the results of the test will not have the desired degree of validity. If the sample of population is large, why not process the instructional material on a batch of literacy classes itself? Indeed, we believe that it is best to test the material on a regular batch of literacy classes and have the materials modified as a result of that experience.

Another problem with judging the effectiveness of instructional materials is presented by the fact that, between the instructional materials and the participants in a literacy class, there is an inevitable intermediary—the instructor. Much depends on his performance in the class. A good teacher succeeds with any type of instructional materials. On the other hand the best materials may be ineffective in the hands of an indifferent teacher. For example, it is not an uncommon fact that some literacy instructors, even those who have been processed through a training course, do not care to go through the instructor's guide. There are some others who do not take the trouble to check students' exercises in the workbook. One wonders how such situations could be remedied.

There is one difficulty of a different type inherent in testing instructional materials for their impact on literacy classes. We have said that the only worthwhile literacy class is a functional literacy class, that is to say, a class composed of participants concerned with improving their attitudes and performance in some aspect of their lives. Now, there is more than one factor involved in effecting change in a person's behaviour. Take a farmers' group. The instructional materials may recommend a particular fertilizer to be used by the farmer. If that fertilizer is not available, then the failure in the change of behaviour cannot be attributed to instructional materials. Also, there are questions of social dynamics involved in social change and these may not be exactly favourable for an individual who has become literate through a literacy class to change his behaviour.

It has been necessary to say all this to warn an evaluation-conscious literacy worker that fool-proof evaluation of instructional materials simply does not exist. But that does not mean that the evaluation of instructional materials should not be attempted. For even if directions may not be available, indications may be available for improving the quality of instructional materials.

However, one type of evaluation that must be undertaken is the expert evaluation. If linguistic and technical experts have not been associated with the preparation of instructional materials, especially the reading texts, the materials must be evaluated and vetted by such experts before using them in literacy classes.

An important mainstay of the evaluation of instructional materials could be the workbooks of the participants, if they have been regularly examined by the instructors. Simple proformas such as the one given in Table 2 on next page could provide a profile of progress for each individual learner and for the whole class.

At the project level these proformas can be put to useful evaluative purposes. Profiles could be developed for each question or lesson for different classes and project areas. If a particular question fetches a low percentage of marks uniformly in all classes of the project, it would indicate the need to recast the lesson in the reading text, the workbook and the instructor's guide. If there is a wide range over which marks in different classes vary for the same questions and the same lessons, there is a presumption that those differences might arise from the varying abilities of instructors of the different groups.

In order to find out if the presumption made above is valid, it is necessary to test instructors in a project area before literacy classes start their work. This test would contain questions similar to those contained in the workbooks, especially those in later lessons. This kind of pre-session test of instructors would serve more than one purpose. It is the author's experience that sometimes an instructor may be nominated for teaching a literacy group because of the power and influence he commands in his community and not because of his ability as an instructor. In any event, we need such a test to see whether the performance of participants in different literacy classes correlates with the abilities of instructors as revealed by the pre-session test.

TABLE 2. *Participants' progress record for the arithmetic workbook*

Class Teacher: .... Village: ....

Lesson no.	Four							Five											Revision lesson 1								
Question no.	1	2	3	4	5	6	T	1	2	3	4	5	6	7	8	9	10	T	1	2	3	4	5	6	7	8	T
Full marks	15	4	8	2	7	3	39	5	10	3	8	1	4	1	9	5	7	53	5	12	15	3	8	4	7	2	56
Marks obtained by each participant:																											
1.................	10	4	2	1	7	2	27	5	5	2	7	1	4	1	8	4	1	38	5	11	12	3	8	2	2	2	45
2.................																											
3.................																											
4.................																											
etc.																											

If the workbooks have been properly examined by the instructors, an end-of-a-spiral test would be a useful additional device to assess the achievements of participants. By itself, one such test lasting for two hours or so would be quite inadequate to assess the achievements of participants on a wide variety of skills in literacy and subject matter. But, along with other data, end-of-the-spiral tests may provide useful insights. Such a test may be the only feasible assessment of the work of both the participants and the instructors, if the instructor has not been examining and marking workbooks.

In the matter of instructor's guides, instructors and, perhaps also, the supervisors are the only sources from which materials for evaluation can be obtained. After a spiral has been completed in the literacy groups, it will be useful to call a meeting of all instructors (and supervisors) to check with them any points or places where they felt dissatisfied with the instructor's guide. A general opinion on a lesson will not do. They should be asked to specify the exact part of a lesson where they felt some difficulty and what kind of difficulty it was. For example, instructors may indicate that it was difficult to follow the lessons on fractions. They should be asked whether the instructor's guide failed to guide them adequately in making the concept of fractions understandable, or whether it was the notion of equivalent fractions itself which was difficult to grasp. Once they are able to specify the difficulty, they may be asked how they would like to recast that particular section. Once they are able to specify the point of difficulty, their suggestions on modifying the particular section should be given all the respect they deserve, because it is they who have to put across the subject matter to the participants.

At the end of the second spiral, an instructor (or a supervisor) should have a *viva voce* examination with participants. In this examination, he should give them a small passage of about 200 words to read. This passage may be of a literacy level comparable to the text they had read in the second spiral, and they should be asked to read it as quickly as they can with comprehension. After that the examiner should ask the participants questions to see if they understood what they had read.

Also, each participant should be asked the following types of questions: Have you done any reading outside of your texts? If so, what did you read? If not, what were the difficulties or blocks in the way of your outside reading? Have you done any writing apart from what you wrote in the course of your classwork? If so, what kind of writing did you do? If not, what hindered you from doing such writing? Have you made any changes in your practical behaviour (on topics related to the subject-matter concerned)? If so, what gave you the inspiration to make these changes? If not, what barred you from profiting from your course?

All the above questions do not impinge directly on the quality of the instructional materials. But if no change came about in the behaviour of the participant as a result of his undergoing a course, then there would be reason to examine the various ingredients of the course to see its short-comings and, especially, to evaluate the role of instructional materials.

Beyond instructional materials

The justification for preparing instructional materials, with all the expertise an instructional materials writer could command, lies only in taking the illiterates to a stage where they will be able to participate fully in modern society, which depends to an amazing degree on reading and writing. But, looking at so many literacy programmes opened with so much fanfare, one is tempted to say, like Shakespeare in another context, that many a literacy project 'is but a walking shadow, a poor player that struts and frets his hour upon the stage and then is heard no more'.

This is so because, for most persons processed through literacy courses, life remains devoid of books or other reading materials. Unless a country embarking on a literacy effort has its own 'book-bowl' and has a mechanism whereby the people at large can share in the book-bowl, there is perhaps no sense in wasting time and effort and scarce resources on literacy projects. If literacy effort is conceived by a country which does not have a commitment to a planned and sustained effort to develop its national brain-power, it is but a tinsel in national life. And developing a nations' brain-power without a continuous flow of reading materials for the people is an idle dream. We will, therefore, speak a few words here on the subject.

There are two parts to a solution of the problem of how to provide reading materials to readers in the cities and rural areas of a country: first, the government of the country should formulate its book development policy; and, second, the government should set up a mechanism for the circulation of books in urban and rural areas through a library service—in addition to other means.

In order to create and enrich a country's book-bowl, the government of the country should have a clear-cut book development policy. Such a policy will have three elements in it: first, utilizing the country's own resources, possibly augmented by international agencies and bilateral agreements; second, entering into regional co-operation with neighbouring countries; and, third, by having a book import policy.

The country's book development resources consist of its writers and translators, printing presses, and private and public publishing agencies. In developing countries, there is hardly any possibility of an author earning his daily bread by taking to writing as a career. Thus, men who have the capacity to write should be identified, encouraged and trained for writing books in their spare time for the new reading public. The encouragement may be in the form of prizes awarded by the government for works that merit recognition. Training is necessary, because those who can write like to re-create the style of their classical writers, rather than writing in order to communicate. Simple writing is not necessarily devoid of charm and beauty, but it is necessary to bring this fact to the attention of those who begin to write for the new literate, and some training seems necessary.

Similarly, translation from one language to another is also an art to be cultivated. Every language has its own idiom, indeed, its own genius, and a literal translation may turn out to be a parody of the original.

Printing requires trained printers, printing machines and paper. Even when printing machinery becomes available through bilateral aid, paper poses a perpetual problem in developing countries. The problem can only be solved by negotiations with international agencies or countries that can afford to supply paper either through donations, or on reduced-cost sales. Even so, there is always a scarcity of paper and it becomes incumbent on governments of developing countries to frame a policy for distributing paper among private and State publishing agencies.

In most developing countries, the government is the biggest publisher. The various ministries of a government produce materials—books and periodicals—which, if written well, could be a very important source of knowledge and information for the people. Unfortunately, many government agencies are manned by university graduates who seldom appreciate the need for simple writing. The same is often the case with writers for private publishing concerns. Moreover, the rising cost of books is putting a great strain on private publishers and, if the global inflation remains unchecked, it may well be that in developing countries private publishers could be pushed out of business.

The second approach to enriching a country's book-bowl might be to enter into regional co-operation with neighbouring countries for mutual benefit. There is, for example, no rational reason why Iran and Afghanistan could not co-operate to increase their book production in science, economics, children's books and many other types of literature. India and Pakistan are other candidates for such co-operation.

Developing countries cannot progress without importing books from countries which are contributing conspicuously to the growth and dissemination of knowledge. Unfortunately, enough foreign exchange is not available to import all the books that are required. Since the last decade or so, some developed countries have permitted a few developing countries to publish cheaper editions of their popular textbooks used in colleges and universities. But, in the first place, the latest editions of such books remain out of such agreements; and, second, books useful to the general public outside the universities are completely forgotten.

All the three ways of enhacing the supply of books to the general public at reasonable price mentioned above require active involvement of the governments in enriching their countries' book-bowls. This can best be done by setting up National Book Councils for co-ordinating activities of writers, of government departments and private publishers; for advising governments on entering into collaboration with neighbouring governments; and for pressing governments to adopt well-considered book development policies. One important item of a desirable book development policy must be a desirable book import policy. This should, as one of the essential parts, discourage, if not exclude altogether, the import of recreational and often just titillating books and magazines, at the cost of literature necessary for national development.

Enriching a country's book-bowl is, of course, only half the story; the other half is to make books available to readers in the towns and villages of a country. The best method for doing so is undoubtedly to set up a network of libraries all over the country. It is common knowledge that men and women who have received a limited education do not go out in search of books; it is the books which have to be sent out to population centres, and even to the homes of potential readers. This will involve some expenditure on the part of the government. But, speaking frankly, it is better not to organize literacy work at all than to let the literacy created through such work to be eroded away in the course of time through lack of its continued use. In the urban areas, where the *per capita* income is greater than in the countryside and where the inducements and even the compulsions of reading are much more than in the countryside, there is scope perhaps for encouraging rental libraries. In the rural areas, the challenge must be met by designing innovative strategies.

I have argued in the above that there are two facets of literacy work— the creation of literacy, and the maintenance of literacy thus created. I have argued that, at the present time, it is an inherent responsibility of governments in developing countries to take up some of the responsibilities of distributing books to their citizens; and, otherwise, to promote the system of dissemination of reading materials by co-ordinating the work of other agencies working in the field. Creating instructional materials by itself would be a self-defeating exercise if we do not go beyond that level and fail to address ourselves to the broader question of maintaining the literacy which is being created in almost all developing countries, primarily through their school systems and sometimes through adult literacy projects.

Summary

The problems of evaluation of instructional materials for their teaching effectiveness and for their impact on the attitude and behaviour of learners have been presented. Especially, the uses of the workbook in developing evaluative information on learner progress, on effectiveness of instructional materials and on instructor's teaching abilities, were discussed. Some comments were included on the evaluation of instructor's guides. The chapter also looked beyond the provision of well-written instructional materials to adult literacy classes, to the need to produce and distribute books needed for those who graduate from functional literacy classes, and those many more who are coming out of the elementary schools in developing countries.